...stallation

CW00522091

by the same author

Electrical Installation Technology 1
Electrical Installation Technology 2
Electrical Installation Technology 3
Multiple Choice Questions in Electrical Installation Work

Worked Examples in Electrical Installation

Maurice L. Lewis

BEd (Hons), MIElecIE
Course 236 Tutor in Electrical Installation Work
at Luton College of Higher Education

Hutchinson

London Melbourne Sydney Auckland Johannesburg

Hutchinson & Co. (Publishers) Ltd

An imprint of the Hutchinson Publishing Group

17—21 Conway Street, London W1P 6JD

Hutchinson Group (Australia) Pty Ltd
PO Box 496, 16—22 Church Street, Hawthorne, Melbourne,
Victoria 3122

Hutchinson Group (NZ) Ltd
32—34 View Road, PO Box 40—086, Glenfield, Auckland 10

Hutchinson Group (SA) (Pty) Ltd
PO Box 337, Bergvlei 2012, South Africa

First published 1984

© Maurice L. Lewis 1984
Illustrations © Hutchinson & Co. (Publishers) Ltd

Set in Press Roman by Allset Composition, London

Printed and bound in Great Britain by
Anchor Brendon Ltd, Tiptree, Essex

British Library Cataloguing in Publication Data
Lewis, Maurice
    Worked examples in electrical installation.
    1. Electrical engineering — Problems,
    exercises etc.
    I. Title
    621.31'042   TK168

ISBN 0 09 156691 6

Contents

Preface

This book has been written for students who are preparing for the City and Guilds of London Institute, Course 236 Part I and Part II Certificates in electrical installation work.

Most of the examples given are based on questions found in volumes 1 and 2 of *Electrical Installation Technology* by the same author. These questions have been divided into *electrical science* and *installation theory* to suit the level of study. Also included are a number of worked examples from recent City and Guilds examination papers.

It is hoped that students will follow the same logical approach in their attempts at similar questions given to them throughout their course study, paying particular attention to layout of work and giving a brief statement of procedure when and where it is necessary. Also important is the need to produce clear, neatly drawn and fully labelled diagrams, a part of students' work often criticized by examination bodies as an area for improvement.

The book uses the latest British Standards Institution, BS 3939 symbols and is completely up to date with its interpretation of the IEE Wiring Regulations for electrical installations. It should be of immense value to all electrical students in the contracting industry.

Acknowledgements

The author wishes to thank the British Standards Institution for permission to use BS 3939 graphical symbols and also the City and Guilds of London Institute for allowing several past examination questions to be reproduced. Answers to these questions are based solely on the author's interpretation and not the examination body.

The author is also grateful to the Institution of Electrical Engineers for allowing reference to be made to its Wiring Regulations. It is hoped that all students of CGLI Course 236 will have a copy of this document.

Part I
Certificate

Electrical science

Note Questions 1–22 are extracted from *Electrical Installation Technology 1*.
Questions 23–50 are additional, based on the course syllabus.

1   Using metric prefixes simplify the following:
  (a)   0.000 5 ampere
  (b)   8 954 000 watts
  (c)   100 000 ohms
  (d)   0.000 000 778 coulomb
  (e)   11 000 volts
  (f)   15.5 milliamperes
  (g)   500 milliwatts
  (h)   0.000 600 9 farad
  (i)   0.000 333 millihenry
  (j)   0.009 8 metre   Ex.1/Vol.1

Solution

(a)   Since 1 mA = 1/1 000 A,

$$\text{then } 0.000\ 5\ \text{A} = \frac{0.000\ 5}{1/1\ 000} = \textbf{0.5 mA.}$$

Alternatively, move the decimal point to
the right three places, thus: 0.000 5A. If
the decimal point was moved six places,
the answer would be **500 μA**. See Figure
1 for reference.
  (b)   Since 1 MW = 1 000 000 W, then
         8 954 000 W = **8.954 MW**
  (c)   100 000 Ω = **100 kΩ**
  (d)   0.000 000 778 C = **778 nC**
  (e)   11 000 V = **11 kV**
  (f)   **15.5 mA**
  (g)   **500 mW**
  (h)   0.000 600 9 F = **600.9 μF**
  (i)   0.000 333 mH = **333 nH**
  (j)   0.009 8 m = **9.8 mm**

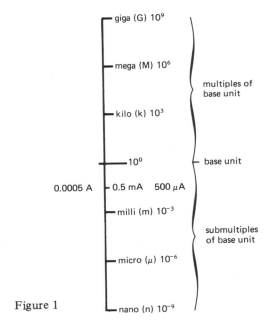

Figure 1

2   Express the following in terms of their
     numerical values, writing after each the
     appropriate unit symbol — as in the first
     example:
  (a)   twenty-four thousand milliamperes -
         24 000 mA
  (b)   forty-three megohms
  (c)   eight hundred thousand microwatts
  (d)   two million voltamperes

(e)   fifty hertz
(f)   four hundred and fifteen volts
(g)   four and three-quarter litres
(h)   one half microhms
(i)   eleven kilovolts
(j)   forty-four milliseconds   Ex.3/Vol.1

Solution

(a)   Note that 24 000 mA = **24 A**
(b)   43 000 000 Ω = **43 MΩ**
(c)   800 000 μW = **800 mW**
(d)   2 000 000 VA = **2 MVA**
(e)   **50 Hz**
(f)   **415 V**
(g)   **4.75 l**
(h)   **0.5 $\mu\Omega$**
(i)   **11 kV**
(j)   **44 ms**

3   Write down an expression for finding:
(a)   *current* when given *charge* and *time*
(b)   *voltage* when given *power* and
       resistance
(c)   *flux density* when given *force, current*
       and *length*
(d)   *volt drop* when given *current* and
       resistance
(e)   *resistivity* when given *resistance, length,*
       and *cross-sectional area*
                                        Ex.4/Q3/Vol.1
Solution

(a)   since $Q = It$ then $I = Q/t$
(b)   since $P = VI$ and $I = V/R$
       then $P = VV/R$ and $V = \sqrt{PR}$
(c)   since $F = Bil$ then $B = F/il$
(d) $V = IR$
(e)   since $R = \dfrac{\rho l}{a}$ then $\rho = Ra/l$

Note   See pages 13 and 14, *Electrical Installation Technology 1*

4   What do the following instruments measure?
(a)   ammeter
(b)   wattmeter
(c)   ohmmeter
(d)   pyrometer
(e)   galvanometer   Ex.4/Q4/Vol.1

Solution

(a)   **current** in amperes
(b)   **power** in watts
(c)   **resistance** in ohms
(d)   **temperature** in therms or degrees Celsius
(e)   **current** but sometimes not calibrated in
       amperes

5   Simplify the following values using prefix
     symbols:
(a)   1 850 W
(b)   0.123 A
(c)   0.005 005 J
(d)   40 992 143 s
(e)   0.035 8 V   Ex.4/Q7/Vol.1

Solution

(a)   1.85 kW
(b)   123 mA
(c)   5 005 μJ
(d)   40.99 Ms
(e)   35.8 mV

6   Rewrite the following using symbols to replace
     the words in italics (i.e. slanting words).
(a)   250 MW is *greater than* 250 kW
(b)   45.59 J is *approximately equal to*
       0.045 6 kWs
(c)   *efficiency* = 79%
(d)   the constant of a circle is *pi*
(e)   1 microfarad *equals* 0.000 001 farad
                                        Ex.4/Q8/Vol.1
Solution

(a)   250 MW $>$ 250 kW
(b)   45.59 J $\approx$ 0.0456 kWs
(c) η = 79%
(d)   the constant of a circle is π
(e)   1 microfarad = 0.000 001 farad

7   Write down the unit for:
(a)   energy
(b)   frequency
(c)   resistivity
(d)   magnetic flux
(e)   luminous flux   Ex.4/Q9/Vol.1

Solution

(a) joule (J)
(b) hertz (Hz)
(c) ohm-metre (Ω-m)
(d) weber (Wb)
(e) lumen (lm)

8 Three resistors of 8 Ω, 12 Ω and 24 Ω respectively, are connected across a 220 V supply. Determine the equivalent resistance of the group: (a) in series and (b) in parallel. In each case, find the power consumed.

Ex.7/Q1/Vol.1

Solution

(a)
$$R = 8 + 12 + 24 \qquad P = \frac{V^2}{R}$$
$$= 44\ \Omega$$
$$= \frac{220 \times 220}{44}$$
$$= 1.1\ \text{kW}$$

(b)
$$\frac{1}{R} = \frac{1}{8} + \frac{1}{12} + \frac{1}{24} \qquad P = \frac{220 \times 220}{4}$$
$$= \frac{6}{24} \qquad\qquad\qquad = 12.1\ \text{kW}$$
$$\therefore R = 4\ \Omega$$

9 Calculate the power dissipated by a 110 V filament lamp having a working resistance of 121 Ω.   Ex.7/Q2/Vol.1

Solution

In practice, lamp wattage is stated on the outer glass envelope of most lamps. While the calculation of power is quite simple, using the expression in Question 8; it should be noted that the lamp's resistance is only about 40 ohms at normal room temperature, i.e. about 25 °C.

$$P = \frac{V^2}{R} = \frac{110 \times 110}{121}$$
$$= 100\ \text{W}$$

10 Determine the supply voltage to a 150 W projector lamp if it takes a current of 0.625 A. Explain what would happen if the supply voltage was increased by 2.5%.

Ex.7/Q3/Vol.1

Solution

In this question:
$$V = \frac{P}{I} = \frac{150}{0.625} = 240\ \text{V}.$$

The maximum voltage variation allowed on a consumer's premises is ± 6% of the declared voltage. However, if the voltage increased by 2.5%, the power of the lamp would increase.

Since
$$P = \frac{V^2}{R}$$

where
$$R = \frac{V}{I} = \frac{240}{0.625} = 384\ \Omega$$

and
$$V = (2.5\% \text{ of } 240\ \text{V}) + 240\ \text{V} = 246\ \text{V}$$

Hence
$$P = \frac{246 \times 246}{384}$$
$$= 157.6\ \text{W}$$

It should be pointed out that lamp manufacturers do not like to see any marked increase in supply voltage since this reduces the expected lamp life.

11 The insulation resistance of a certain cable is 500 MΩ. What leakage current is likely to flow when the cable's insulation is subject to a stress voltage of 500 V?   Ex.7/Q4/Vol.1

Solution

The cable has a very good insulation resistance value and consequently the leakage current is very small, i.e.
$$I = \frac{V}{R} = \frac{500}{500} \times 10^{-6}$$
$$= 0.000\ 001\ \text{A or } 1\ \mu\text{A}$$

It should be noted that the longer the cable run, the less its insulation resistance value will be: its value is inversely proportional to its length. In other words, the cross-sectional area of the cable's sheath (i.e. circumference $\times$ length) increases with length of run.

12 The energy used by a resistive load in 14 hours is 847 MWh. What is the current taken by the load if the supply voltage is 11 kV?

Ex.7/Q5/Vol.1

Solution

In this question, first divide the 14 hours into the 847 MWh (megawatthours). Thus:

$$P = \frac{MWh}{h} = \frac{847}{14} = \textbf{60.5 MW}$$

From this:

$$I = \frac{P}{V} = \frac{60.5 \times 10^6}{11 \times 10^3} = \textbf{5 500 A}$$

13 A cable has a total resistance of 0.6 Ω. When it carries a current of 60 A, determine:

(a)   its volt drop
(b)   its power loss
(c)   the energy consumed over 24 hours

Ex.7/Q6/Vol.1

Solution

(a)   As pointed out earlier, volt drop is found by:

$$V = IR = 60 \times 0.6 = \textbf{36 V}$$

(b)   Power loss is found by:

$$P = I^2R = 60 \times 60 \times 0.6 = 2\ 160 \text{ W or}$$
2.16 kW

(c)   Energy used is found by:

$$W = Pt = 2.16 \times 24 = \textbf{51.84 kWh}$$

14 Which of the following conductors has the least electrical resistance?

(a)   a short copper conductor of 2.5 mm²
(b)   a short copper conductor of 1.5 mm²
(c)   a long copper conductor of 1.5 mm²
(d)   a long copper conductor of 2.5 mm²

Ex.7/Q7/Vol.1

Solution

This is a relatively easy question if students can remember resistance and its dependence on dimensions (see 'Resistance factors', page 45, *Electrical Installation Technology 1*). The conductor with the least electrical resistance will be the shortest and thickest one, that is (a).

15 Calculate the total current of six 40 W, 240 V lamps connected in parallel.   Ex.7/Q8/Vol.1

Solution

This is another simple question based on the power expression used before, i.e. $P = VI$. From this:

$$I = \frac{P}{V} = \frac{6 \times 40}{240} = \textbf{1 A}$$

Note that each lamp takes 0.166 A.

16 Calculate the total wattage of six 100 W, 240 V lamps connected (a) in series and (b) in parallel.

Ex.7/Q9/Vol.1

Solution

(a)   In this arrangement, each lamp does not receive its full working voltage, but only one-sixth of the supply voltage, i.e. 40 V. Since each lamp has a working resistance of:

$$R = \frac{V^2}{P} = \frac{240 \times 240}{100} = 576\ \Omega$$

then power of each lamp is:

$$P = \frac{V^2}{R} = \frac{40 \times 40}{576} = 2.777 \text{ W}$$

total wattage is: $6 \times 2.777 = \textbf{16.66 W}$

(b)   In this arrangement, each lamp is connected across the 240 V supply and all lamp wattages can be added together, i.e. **600 W**. Notice that

$$\frac{600}{16.66} = 36 \text{ also } \frac{240}{40} = 6.$$

The voltage squared is an important factor since $6^2 = 36$. Arrangement (b) gives 36 times more power.

17 The resistance of a 60 W lamp is 960 Ω. What is the current taken by the lamp?

Ex.7/Q10/Vol.1

Solution

Since $P = I^2R$ then:

$$I = \sqrt{\frac{P}{R}} = \sqrt{\frac{60}{960}} = \textbf{0.25 A}$$

Further calculation will show that the lamp is 240 V.

18 The primary winding of a transformer consists of 400 turns, its secondary voltage is 240 volts and its primary current is 8 amperes. Determine the primary voltage, secondary turns and secondary current if its transformation ratio is 1:1.73.   Ex.9/Q1/Vol.1

Solution

First, students must remember that the transformation ratio of a transformer is given by:

$$\frac{V_p}{V_s} = \frac{N_p}{N_s} = \frac{I_s}{I_p}$$

where V_p is primary volts
V_s is secondary volts
N_p is primary turns
N_s is secondary turns
I_p is primary current
I_s is secondary current

Since each ratio = 1:1.73 (step-up)

then

$$\frac{V_p}{240} = \frac{1}{1.73}$$

therefore

$$V_p = \frac{240}{1.73}$$

$$= 138.7 \text{ V}$$

Similarly:

$$\frac{400}{N_s} = \frac{1}{1.73}$$

and

$$N_s = 400 \times 1.73$$

$$= 692 \text{ turns}$$

Also:

$$\frac{I_s}{8} = \frac{1}{1.73}$$

and

$$I_s = \frac{8}{1.73}$$

$$= 4.62 \text{ A}$$

19 A transformer has a turns ratio of 250:20. What is the secondary current if the primary current is 10 A?   Ex.9/Q2/Vol.1

Solution

The first thing to note is that the transformer is a step-down one with 250 turns on its primary and 20 turns on its secondary. The transformation ratio is 12.5:1 and from the previous question (Question 18):

$$\frac{I_s}{I_p} = 12.5$$

Thus:

$$I_s = I_p \times 12.5$$

$$= 10 \times 12.5$$

$$= 125 \text{ A}$$

20 An auto-transformer has 480 turns on its primary winding. If it is supplied with 240 volts and its secondary voltage is 24 volts, how many turns has its secondary winding?
                    Ex.9/Q3/Vol.1

Solution

As indicated, an auto-transformer is one with only one winding as shown in Figure 2. It will be noticed that the secondary voltage is from a tapping point on the winding and since the ratio:

$$\frac{V_p}{V_s} = \frac{240}{24} = 10$$

then

$$\frac{N_p}{N_s} = 10$$

therefore:

$$N_s = \frac{N_p}{10} = \frac{480}{10} = 48 \text{ turns}$$

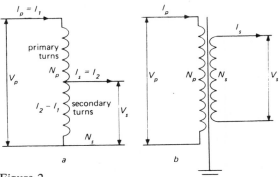

Figure 2

21 Describe the principles of transformer action, and write down the expression for the transformation ratio.   Ex.9/Q5/Vol.1

Solution

The answer to this question can be found in *Electrical Installation Technology 1*, Installation Circuits 2, pages 59–62. Briefly, a double-wound transformer operates on the principle of mutual induction, i.e. when an a.c. supply is fed into the primary winding of the transformer, the current that flows produces an alternating magnetic flux in the iron core. This flux induces not only a back e.m.f. in the primary winding but also an e.m.f. in the secondary winding. The voltage induced in the secondary winding depends upon the number of turns of this winding. Since both windings are linked by the same magnetic flux, their induced e.m.f.s will be proportional to the number of turns in each coil.

See the solution to Question 18 for the transformation ratio.

22 Determine the power factor of an inductive circuit supplied at 240 V and taking a current of 30 A. Assume the load has an output of 4.5 kW and efficiency of 86%.

Ex.10/Q6/Vol.1

Solution

Reference should be made to pages 70–1 of *Electrical Installation Technology 1* where power factor is explained. It will be seen that:

$$\text{p.f.} = \frac{P}{VI}$$

where P is the input power in watts

Since efficiency = $\dfrac{\text{output}}{\text{input}}$

the input power = $\dfrac{\text{output}}{\text{efficiency}}$

$$= \frac{4\ 500}{86} \times 100$$

$$= 5233 \text{ W (approx.)}$$

therefore

$$\text{p.f.} = \frac{5233}{240 \times 30}$$

$$= \textbf{0.727 lagging}$$

23 (a) Explain the following terms: frequency; periodic time; maximum value; r.m.s. value.

(b) With the aid of a diagram, explain how a.c. is produced from a simple single loop generator.

Solution

(a) *frequency* this describes the number of cycles completed in a time of one second (usually). Its derived SI unit is called the *hertz*.

periodic time this is the time taken to complete one cycle and the relationship between itself and frequency is given by the expression:

$$T = \frac{1}{f}$$

maximum value this is the highest point (instantaneous point) reached by an a.c. waveform often called the *peak* value.

r.m.s. value this is called the *root mean square* value or *effective* value of an a.c. waveform, be it voltage or current. Its value can be derived from the expression:

$$V_{\text{r.m.s.}} = 0.707 \times V_{\text{max}}$$

or

$$I_{\text{r.m.s.}} = 0.707 \times I_{\text{max}}$$

(b) The answer to this part can be found on page 57 of *Electrical Installation Technology 1*. Briefly, the loop shown in Figure 3 has to be rotated for the conductor to produce an induced e.m.f. This is brought about by *flux cutting* as the conductor rotates through the magnetic field. Current in the external circuit will only flow if the circuit is complete through some form of load. Apply Fleming's right-hand rule to ascertain the current direction.

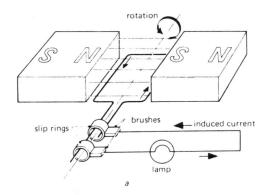

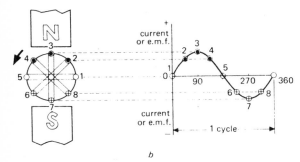

Figure 3 (a) *Single loop generator*
(b) *Rotating conductor*

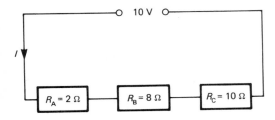

Figure 4

24   With reference to Figure 4 determine the
following:
(a)   equivalent circuit resistance
(b)   current flowing in the circuit
(c)   quantity of electricity over a period of
6 hours
(d)   potential difference across each resistor
(e)   power consumed by each resistor and
total power
(f)   energy used in the circuit over a period
of 6 hours

Solution

(a) $R_e = R_A + R_B + R_C$
$= 2 + 8 + 10$
$= \textbf{20 } \boldsymbol{\Omega}$

(b) $I = \dfrac{V}{R_e}$
$= \dfrac{10}{20}$
$= \textbf{0.5 A}$

(c) $Q = I \times t$
$= 0.5 \times 6 \times 3\ 600$
$= \textbf{10 800 C}$

(d) $V_A = I \times R_A$
$= 0.5 \times 2$
$= \textbf{1 V}$
$V_B = I \times R_B$
$= 0.5 \times 8$
$= \textbf{4 V}$
$V_C = I \times R_C$
$= 0.5 \times 10$
$= \textbf{5 V}$

(e) $P_A = V_A \times I$
$= 1 \times 0.5$
$= \textbf{0.5 W}$
$P_B = V_B \times I$
$= 4 \times 0.5$
$= \textbf{2.0 W}$
$P_C = V_C \times I$
$= 5 \times 0.5$
$= \textbf{2.5 W}$
$P = P_A + P_B + P_C$
$= 0.5 + 2.0 + 2.5$
$= \textbf{5 W}$

(f) $W = P \times t$
$= 5 \times 6 \times 3\ 600$
$= \textbf{108 000 J}$

25 From the answers given in Question 24 express:
   (a) equivalent resistance in terms of kilo-ohms
   (b) current in terms of milliamperes
   (c) quantity of electricity in terms of mega-coulombs
   (d) energy in terms of megajoules and kilo-watthours

Solution

(a) Since 1 kΩ = 1 000 Ω

   then $20\ \Omega = \dfrac{20}{1\ 000} = \mathbf{0.02\ k\Omega}$

(b) Since 1 mA $= \dfrac{1}{1\ 000}\ A$

   then 0.5 A $= \dfrac{0.5}{1/1\ 000} = \mathbf{500\ mA}$

(c) Since 1 MC = 1 000 000 C

   then 10 800 C $= \dfrac{10\ 800}{1\ 000\ 000} = \mathbf{0.0108\ MC}$

(d) Since 1 MJ = 1 000 000 J

   then 108 000 J $= \dfrac{108\ 000}{1\ 000\ 000} = \mathbf{0.108\ MJ}$

   Also:

   since 1 kWh = 3.6 MJ

   then 0.108 MJ $= \dfrac{0.108}{3.6} = \mathbf{0.03\ kWh}$

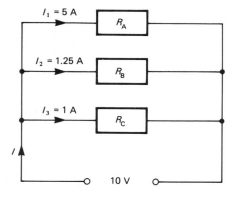

Figure 5

26 With reference to Figure 5 determine the following:
   (a) equivalent circuit resistance

(b) value of each resistor
(c) power consumed by each resistor and total power
(d) energy used in the circuit over a period of 6 hours

Solution

(a) $R_e = \dfrac{V}{I} = \dfrac{10}{7.25} = \mathbf{1.379\ \Omega}$

(b) $R_A = \dfrac{V}{I} = \dfrac{10}{5} = \mathbf{2\ \Omega}$

   $R_B = \dfrac{V}{I} = \dfrac{10}{1.25} = \mathbf{8\ \Omega}$

   $R_C = \dfrac{V}{I} = \dfrac{10}{1} = \mathbf{10\ \Omega}$

(c) $P_A = I^2R = 5 \times 5 \times 2 = \mathbf{50\ W}$
   $P_B = I^2R = 1.25 \times 1.25 \times 8 = \mathbf{12.5\ W}$
   $P_C = I^2R = 1 \times 1 \times 10 = \mathbf{10\ W}$
   Total power (P) = $P_A + P_B + P_C$ = 50 + 12.5 + 10 = **72.5 W**. (Note that P = $V \times I$ = 10 × 7.25 = 72.5 W)

(d) $W = P \times t = 72.5 \times 6 \times 3\ 600$
       = 1 566 000 J = **1.566 MJ**

27 With reference to Questions 24 and 26, state several comparisons between both circuits.

Solution

(a) In the series circuit the current is common to all the resistors, whereas in the parallel circuit it is the supply voltage which is common across all the resistors.
(b) In the series circuit the sum of the internal p.d.s add up to the supply voltage, whereas in the parallel circuit it is the sum of the branch currents which adds up to the total current flowing in the circuit.
(c) The equivalent resistance of the parallel circuit is smaller than the smallest value resistor connected, whereas in the series circuit the total resistance is the sum of the individual resistors.
(d) Power consumption is greater in the parallel circuit than in the series circuit.

28 A battery consisting of nine primary cells is connected to an external resistance of 10 Ω. If each cell has an e.m.f. of 1.5 V and internal resistance 0.45 Ω, determine the circuit current and volt drop across the 10 Ω resistor when the cells are arranged in (a) series, (b) parallel and (c) three sets in parallel, each consisting of three cells in series.

Solution

Figure 6 illustrates the circuit connections.

(a) $I = \dfrac{nE}{R + nr}$

where n is the number of cells

R is the external resistor

r is the internal resistance of each cell

Thus $I = \dfrac{9 \times 1.5}{10 + (9 \times 0.45)}$

$= \mathbf{0.961\ A}$

Also $V = I \times R$

$= 0.961 \times 10$

$= \mathbf{9.61\ V}$

(b) $I = \dfrac{E}{R + r/9}$

$= \dfrac{1.5}{10 + 0.05}$

$= \mathbf{0.149\ A}$

$V = I \times R$

$= 0.149 \times 10$

$= \mathbf{1.49\ V}$

(c) $I = \dfrac{n/3 \times E}{R + r}$

where $r = \dfrac{3 \times 0.45}{3}$

$I = \dfrac{3 \times 1.5}{10 + 0.45}$

$= \mathbf{0.43\ A}$

$V = I \times R$

$= 0.43 \times 10$

$= \mathbf{4.3\ V}$

Note The series cell connections provide the highest battery voltage, but when current flows a high internal

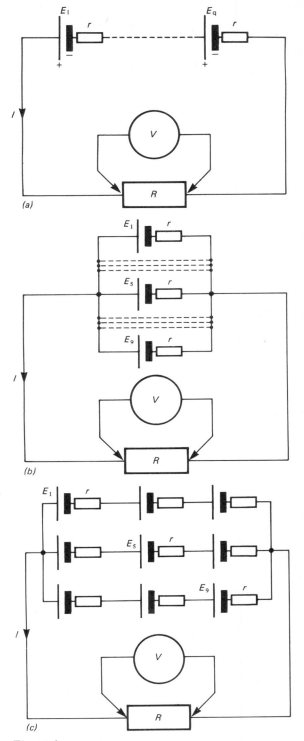

(a)

(b)

(c)

Figure 6

volt drop occurs (approximately 4 V). The parallel arrangement produces the lowest internal volt drop, only 0.01 V, but suffers by having a low battery voltage. In the series/parallel connection a compromise is found; battery voltage is reasonable and the internal volt drop of 0.2 V is due to the internal resistance being equivalent to one cell.

29 Briefly state the main differences between Planté, tubular and flat plate lead-acid cells.

Solution

The main differences between the cells are in the positive plates, the containers which are used and also their expected life.

The Planté positive plate is made of pure lead. A number of thin vertical lamelles provide a large active surface area which gives a high capacity and continuous regeneration of active material from the basic metal. This type of cell gives 100% capacity throughout its very long life. The containers used for Planté cells are transparent styrene acrylonitrite in order to allow visual inspection to be made of electrolyte levels.

In the tubular positive plate type, the tubes are made from terylene or other similar material fitted over cast lead alloy spines attached to a common metallic busbar at the top of the plate. The space between the lead spine and the tubing is filled with lead oxide which is retained within the tube by a plastic plug. In this way the active material is maintained within the conducting spines during the cell's charge and discharge. In practice, these cells give high power for a minimum volume and are very robust. Containers may also be of transparent plastic for maintenance reasons but the cell's life expectancy is not as good as the Planté type.

In the flat plate type cells, lead oxide paste is pressed into a metallic grid which serves the purpose of retaining the active material as well as a conducting medium for the passage of current. The positive plate of these pasted cells is similar to the negative plate of the Planté and tubular cells but their containers may again be transparent to allow visual inspection to be made. For harder use, containers are available made from hard rubber.

30 Determine the efficiency of an electric kettle rated at 3 kW/240 V when it contains 1 litre of water. The change of temperature from cold to boiling point is 80 °C and the time taken to boil is 2 minutes 10 seconds. Assume the specific heat capacity of water to be 4.2 kJ/kg °C and that 1 litre = 1 kg.

Solution

Heat energy required (output):
$$W_o = mc(\theta_2 - \theta_1)$$
$$= 1 \times 4200 \times 80$$
$$= 0.336 \text{ MJ}$$

since 1 kWh = 3.6 MJ then
$$W_o = \frac{0.336}{3.6} \text{ kWh}$$
$$= 0.093 \text{ kWh}$$

Heat energy required (input):
$$W_i = Pt$$
$$= 3 \times \frac{130}{3\,600}$$
$$= 0.108 \text{ kWh}$$

$$\% \text{ efficiency} = \frac{\text{output}}{\text{input}} \times 100$$
$$= \frac{0.093 \times 100}{0.108}$$
$$= 86\%$$

31 Figure 7 shows the connections of four capacitors, determine:
(a)   the equivalent capacitance of the circuit
(b)   the total charge for the p.d. given
(c)   the total energy stored

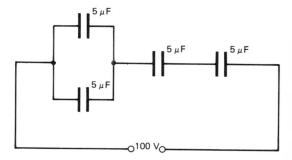

Figure 7

Solution

(a) In the parallel branch the equivalent
     capacitance is $C = C_1 + C_2$.

Thus $C = 5 + 5 = 10\ \mu F$

The equivalent capacitance of the whole
circuit is:

$$\frac{1}{C_e} = \frac{1}{C} + \frac{1}{C_3} + \frac{1}{C_4}$$

$$= \frac{1}{10} + \frac{1}{5} + \frac{1}{5}$$

$$= \frac{1 + 2 + 2}{10}$$

$$= \frac{5}{10}\ \mu F$$

$$C_e = \frac{10}{5}$$

$$= 2\ \mu F$$

(b) The total charge is given by the expression
     $Q = CV$

Thus $Q = 2 \times 10^{-6} \times 100$

$$= 200\ \mu C$$

(c) The total energy is found by the expres-
     sion $W = \frac{1}{2}CV^2$

Thus $W = \frac{1}{2} \times 2 \times 10^{-6} \times 100 \times 100$

$$= 0.01\ J$$

32 Figure 8 represents an impedance triangle.
     (a) Write down an expression for finding Z
          and determine its ohmic value.

(b) State meanings for the following terms:
     impedance; reactance and resistance.

Solution

(a) $Z = \sqrt{R^2 + X^2}$

$Z = \sqrt{20^2 + 40^2}$

$= \sqrt{400 + 1\ 600}$

$= \sqrt{2\ 000}$

$= 44.72\ \Omega$

(b) *Impedance* This is the ratio of voltage to
     current (V/I) in r.m.s. terms for a.c.
     quantities. Since it is represented by the
     hypotenuse in Figure 8 it will be the
     largest value in the circuit or total oppo-
     sition to current flow.
     Reactance In a.c. circuits it is the oppo-
     sition to current flow by components
     possessing inductance or capacitance
     such as stator windings, transformers,
     lamp ballasts (which possess inductance)
     or capacitors (which possess capacitance).
     Resistance The property of a material
     to resist the flow of current through a
     circuit such as a resistor.

33 With reference to the balanced system in
     Figure 9 determine:
     (a) the phase current in the delta connection
     (b) the phase current in the star connection
     (c) the phase voltage in the delta connection
     (d) the phase voltage in the star connection

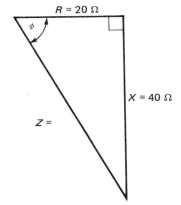

Figure 8

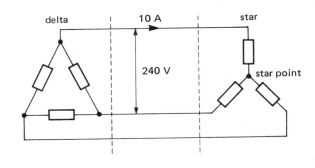

Figure 9

Solution

(a) $I_P = \dfrac{I_L}{\sqrt{3}} = \dfrac{10}{1.732} = $ **5.77 A**

(b) $I_P = I_L = $ **10 A**

(c) $V_P = V_L = $ **240 V**

(d) $V_P = \dfrac{V_L}{\sqrt{3}} = \dfrac{240}{1.732} = $ **138.6 V**

Note I_P is phase current
$\quad\;\; I_L$ is line current
$\quad\;\; V_P$ is phase voltage
$\quad\;\; V_L$ is line voltage
$\quad\;\; \sqrt{3} = 1.732$

34 (a) With reference to Figure 8, the angle (ϕ) shown can represent power factor. If the reactance is inductive, determine the power factor, stating whether it is *unity, lagging* or *leading*.

(b) Write down a more exact expression for finding power factor and provide a brief explanation as to its importance in a.c. circuits.

Solution

(a) Having already worked out Z to be 44.72 Ω, power factor ($\cos \phi$) can be determined using trigonometry, i.e.:

$$\cos \phi = \frac{\text{adjacent}}{\text{hypotenuse}} = \frac{R}{Z} = \frac{20}{44.72}$$

$$= 0.447$$

Hence power factor is 0.447 lagging (since reactance is inductive).

(b) Power factor is the ratio of

$$\frac{\text{active power} \;\; (P)}{\text{apparent power (VI)}}$$

An explanation of power factor is given in *Electrical Installation Technology 2*, page 42.

The active power and voltage in a system are often fixed, consequently any power less than unity (1) will cause more current to flow in the system than otherwise necessary. For this reason, supply authorities penalize consumers who have low power factors, i.e. those below 0.8 lagging, because it means that larger cables and switchgear need to be installed to meet the consumer's load conditions.

35 (a) Show by diagram how an induced e.m.f. is created using a permanent magnet, coil and millivoltmeter.

(b) State a number of principles associated with (a) above.

(c) What is the value of induced e.m.f. in a conductor 0.4 m long if it moves at a velocity of 20 m/s at right angles to a magnetic field of strength 2.5 T?

Solution

(a) See Figure 10.

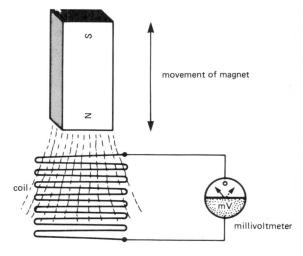

Figure 10

(b) (i) An e.m.f. is induced if either the magnet or the coil is moved relative to each other.

(ii) The magnitude of the induced e.m.f. depends on the rate at which either the magnet or coil is moved towards each other.

(iii) The polarity of the induced e.m.f. depends on the polarity of the permanent magnet and on the direction of movement.

(c) An expression for finding induced e.m.f.
is $e = Blv$
where B is the magnetic flux density in
tesla (T)
l is the effective length in
metres (m)
v is the velocity in metre/second
(m/s)
Thus $e = 2.5 \times 0.4 \times 20$
$= \textbf{20 V}$

Solution
The application of the rule is as suggested,
the induced current direction shown by a
cross denoting current going in and a *dot*
denoting current coming out, as shown in
Figure 11(b).

36 Using the model of Fleming's right-hand rule
in Figure 11(a), determine the induced current
directions in the four conductors.

37 (a) Make a sketch of a simple screwjack.
(b) The screw of a screwjack has 500 threads
per metre. If its handle is 0.25 m in
length what is its movement ratio?
(c) If the screwjack had an efficiency of 32%,
what load could be lifted for an applied
effort of 95 N?

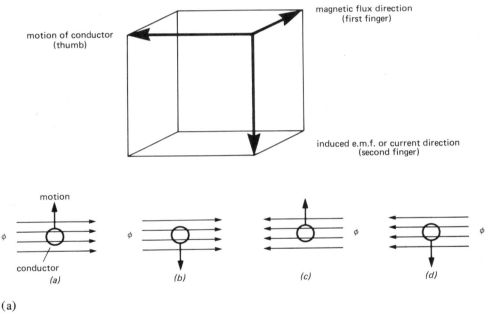

Figure 11 (a)

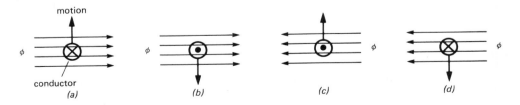

Figure 11 (b)

Solution

(a)   See Figure 12.

(b)   movement ratio (MR)

$$= \frac{2\pi \times \text{length of handle}}{\text{screw pitch}}$$

$$= \frac{2 \times 3.142 \times 0.25}{1/500}$$

$$= \frac{1.571}{0.002}$$

$$= \textbf{785.5}$$

(c)   load = effort × force ratio (FR)
       and FR = MR × efficiency

Thus load = $95 \times 785.5 \times \dfrac{32}{100}$

$$= \textbf{23.88 kN}$$

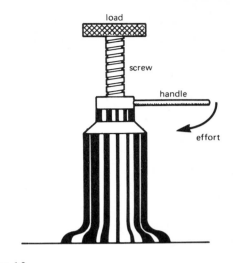

Figure 12

38   Make a neat circuit diagram of a simple battery
charger, comprising double-wound transformer,
bridge rectifier, ammeter, regulator and battery
being charged.

Solution

See Figure 13.

39   What is meant by the following terms?
(a)   oxidation
(b)   electrolysis
(c)   corrosion

Solution

(a)   *Oxidation* is the combination of oxygen
       with a substance such as a metal. It gives
       the metal an oxide skin which protects it
       to some extent from corrosion –
       aluminium alloy is a good example of this.
(b)   *Electrolysis* is the term given to the
       chemical decomposition of certain sub-
       stances, particularly liquid electrolytes,
       when a direct current is passed through
       the substance. Basically, the substances

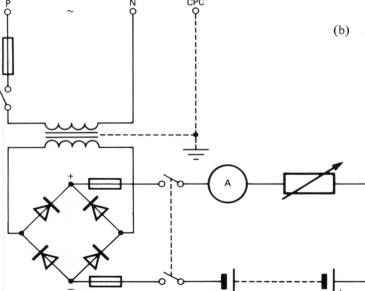

Figure 13

are ionized into electrically charged *ions* and when current is passed through them via electrodes they move towards the attracting electrode where they give up their charge to become uncharged atoms; they may be liberated or deposited on to the electrode or they may react chemically with the electrode or the electrolyte (or both) according to their chemical nature.

(c) *Corrosion* may be described as the chemical or electrochemical reaction of a metal with its environment resulting in the metal's progressive destruction whereupon it reverts back to its natural oxide state. All metal surfaces have an electrical potential created by differences on their surfaces, such as flaws, impurities, acidity etc. The electrochemical reaction is such that at the high potential *anodic* area an oxidation process occurs which results in a loss of electrons and release of positively charged metal ions going into solution. A simultaneous reduction process occurs at the low potential *cathodic* area on the metal resulting in a gain of electrons. The process causes metal ions to leave the surface at the point of their discharge and corrosion of the metal takes place.

40   With reference to Figure 14, determine:
(a)   the supply current
(b)   the volt drop across each load A, B, C and D.
   Assume the cable used has a resistance of 0.1 ohm/1 000 metre.

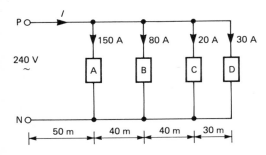

Figure 14

Solution

(a)   The supply current is the addition of the branch currents, i.e.:

$$I = I_A + I_B + I_C + I_D$$
$$= 150 + 80 + 20 + 30$$
$$= \textbf{280 A}$$

(b)   Since volt drop $V = I \times R$, then volt drop in cables from origin to load A is:

$$V = 280 \times \left(2 \times 50 \times \frac{0.1}{1\,000}\right)$$
$$= 280 \times 0.01$$
$$= \textbf{2.8 V}$$

volt drop in cables between loads A and B is:

$$V = 130 \times \left(2 \times 40 \times \frac{0.1}{1\,000}\right)$$
$$= 130 \times 0.008$$
$$= \textbf{1.04 V}$$

volt drop in cables between loads B and C is:

$$V = 50 \times \left(2 \times 40 \times \frac{0.1}{1\,000}\right)$$
$$= 50 \times 0.008$$
$$= \textbf{0.4 V}$$

volt drop in cables between loads C and D is:

$$V = 30 \times \left(2 \times 30 \times \frac{0.1}{1\,000}\right)$$
$$= 30 \times 0.006$$
$$= \textbf{0.18 V}$$

Note   It should be pointed out that the terminal p.d. for load A is $240 - 2.8 = 237.2$ V; for load B it is $237.2 - 1.04 = 236.16$ V; for load C it is $236.16 - 0.4 = 235.76$ V; and for load D it is $235.76 - 0.18 = 235.58$ V. At load D the permissible minimum terminal voltage is 234 V (i.e. a 6 V maximum volt drop allowed from a 240 V supply — see IEE Wiring Regulations, Reg. 522.8)

41 A coil has a resistance of 300 ohm at 0 °C. If its resistance is found to increase to 330 ohm at 25 °C, what is the temperature coefficient of resistance?

Solution

An expression for the temperature coefficient of resistance is given on page 45 of *Electrical Installation Technology 1* (see also Figure 53 on page 46).

The expression is:

$$\alpha = \frac{R_t - R_0}{R_0 t}$$

where R_t is the resistance at 25 °C
R_0 is the resistance at 0 °C
t is the temperature at 25 °C

$$\alpha = \frac{330 - 300}{300 \times 25}$$

$$= 0.004 \ \Omega/\Omega/°C \text{ at } 0 \ °C$$

Note Copper has this value.

42 A piece of resistance wire 10 m long and of 10 mm² c.s.a. passes a current of 5 A when connected to a 240 V supply. What is the resistivity of the wire?

Solution

Since $R = \dfrac{V}{I}$

$$= \frac{240}{5}$$

$$= 48 \ \Omega$$

And also $R = \dfrac{\rho \times l}{A}$

where R is the resistance in Ω
ρ is the resistivity in $\mu\Omega$m
A is the cross-sectional area in mm²
l is the length in m

then by transposition of formula:

$$\rho = \frac{R \times A}{l}$$

$$= \frac{48 \times 10 \times 10^6}{10 \times 10^6}$$

$$= 48 \ \mu\Omega\text{m}$$

Note Area converted into m² by 10^6 factor

43 A load of 60 kg is placed 100 mm from the fulcrum of a lever. What force is required on the other side of the lever which is 0.4 m from the fulcrum in order to raise the load?

Solution

This question relates to the *principle of moments* which states that in any system which is in equilibrium (i.e. in balance), the total clockwise moment equals the total anticlockwise moment.

Thus

$$F_1 \times d_1 = F_2 \times d_2$$

and

$$F_1 = \frac{F_2 \times d_2}{d_1}$$

where F_1 is the force of the clockwise movement
d_1 is the distance of the clockwise moment
F_2 is the force of the anticlockwise moment
d_2 is the distance of the anticlockwise moment

See Figure 15.

therefore

$$F_1 = \frac{60 \times 100}{400} \times 9.81$$

$$= 147.15 \text{ N}$$

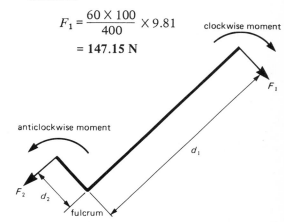

Figure 15

44 (a) With the aid of a diagram illustrate how a conductor carrying current is made to move out of the influence of a permanent magnetic field.

(b) A conductor 50 mm in length lies at right angles to a magnetic field of field strength 25 T. Calculate the force on the conductor when it carries a current of 10 A.

(c) Give *two* practical examples of (a) above.

Solution

(a) See Figure 16.

(b) Force on the conductor is given by:

$$F = B \times l \times I \text{ newtons}$$

where B is the magnetic field strength (T)
I is the current in the conductor (A)
l is the length of conductor (m)

thus $F = 25 \times 0.05 \times 10$

$= \mathbf{12.5\ N}$

(c) Motor operation
Instrument operation

45 What is meant by the following terms in relation to circuit fuselinks?

(a) current rating
(b) rated voltage
(c) rated minimum fusing current
(d) fusing factor
(e) breaking capacity rating

Solution

(a) This is a current less than the minimum fusing current, stated by a manufacturer as the current a fuselink will carry continuously without deteriorating.

(b) This is the voltage assigned by a manufacturer to indicate the nominal system voltage with which a fuselink is associated.

(c) This is the current stated as being that required to cause the fuselink to operate in a specified time under prescribed conditions.

(d) This is the ratio (being greater than unity) of rated minimum fusing current to the current rating.

(e) This is the prospective current (see Question 87(c)) stated by the manufacturer as the greatest current value that may be associated with the fuselink under prescribed conditions of voltage, power factor or time.

46 With reference to Figure 17, calculate the current in each part of the circuit.

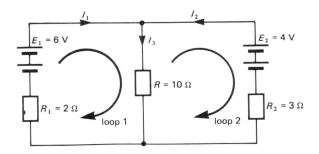

Figure 17

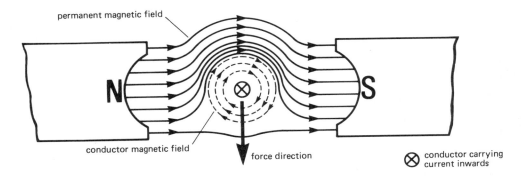

Figure 16

Solution

Figure 17 shows that there are three currents to be found. One method is to apply Kirchhoff's Laws as shown below.

Kirchhoff's first Law is concerned with the total current flowing towards a junction is equal to the current flowing away from that junction. In Figure 17 it is not too difficult to see that $I_3 = I_1 + I_2$. It is these currents that we have to find.

Kirchhoff's second Law concerns a closed circuit and states that the algebraic sum of the p.d.s (IR drops) in each part of the circuit is equal to the resultant e.m.f. in the circuit, i.e. $E_1 - E_2 = I_1 R_1 - I_2 R_2$. Notice that $E_1 > E_2$.

Consider loop 1 for the current I_1

$$E_1 = I_1 R_1 + R(I_1 + I_2)$$
$$6 = 2I_1 + 10(I_1 + I_2)$$
$$6 = 12I_1 + 10I_2 \tag{i}$$

Consider loop 2 for current I_2

$$E_2 = I_2 R_2 + R(I_1 + I_2)$$
$$4 = 3I_2 + 10(I_1 + I_2)$$
$$4 = 10I_1 + 13I_2 \tag{ii}$$

Now multiply (i) by 5 and (ii) by 6

Thus (i) becomes:

$$30 = 60I_1 + 50I_2 \tag{iii}$$

And (ii) becomes:

$$24 = 60I_1 + 78I_2 \tag{iv}$$

Now subtract (iv) from (iii):

$$30 = 60I_1 + 50I_2$$
$$24 = 60I_1 + 78I_2$$
$$6 = 0 - 28I_2$$

Therefore $I_2 = -\dfrac{6}{28} = -0.214$ A

Substitute I_2 in (i) above to find I_1

Thus (i) becomes

$$6 = 12I_1 + (10 \times (-0.214))$$
$$= 12I_1 - 2.14$$
$$8.14 = 12I_1$$
$$I_1 = \frac{8.14}{12} = 0.678 \text{ A}$$

Since $I_3 = I_1 + I_2$

$$I_3 = 0.678 + (-0.214) = 0.464 \text{ A}$$

47 A length of conduit 3 m long is cut into three pieces, the second piece is twice as long as the first while the third piece is 40 cm shorter than the first. If 20 cm is allowed for wastage, find the length of the three pieces.

Solution

The solution to this question can be found using algebra, taking the first piece as x, the second piece as $2x$ and the third piece as $x - 40$. The total length of these pieces is 20 cm short of 3 m, i.e. 280 cm. Thus

$$x + 2x + (x - 40) = 280$$
$$4x - 40 = 280$$
$$4x = 320$$
$$\text{First piece } x = \frac{320}{4}$$
$$= 80 \text{ cm}$$
$$\text{Second piece } 2x = 160 \text{ cm}$$
$$\text{Third piece } x - 40 = 40 \text{ cm}$$

48 Find the volume of a round and hollow copper busbar 15 m in length having internal and external diameters of 5.5 cm and 6.0 cm respectively.

Solution

$$\text{Volume} = \text{area of end (thickness of tube)}$$
$$\times \text{ length}$$
$$= \left(\pi \frac{d_1{}^2}{4} - \pi \frac{d_2{}^2}{4} \right) \times 1$$

where $d_1 = 6.0$ cm

$d_2 = 5.5$ cm

$$\text{Volume} = \frac{\pi l}{4}(d_1{}^2 - d_2{}^2)$$
$$= \frac{\pi l}{4}(d_1 + d_2)(d_1 - d_2)$$
$$= \frac{3.142 \times 1\,500 \times 11.5 \times 0.5}{4}$$
$$= 6\,775 \text{ cm}^3 \text{ (approx.)}$$
$$= 0.006\,775 \text{ m}^3$$

49 A domestic consumer's previous and present quarterly meter readings are 58 142 and 59 361 respectively. If each unit of electricity costs 4.83p and the standing charge is £6.37, what is his quarterly bill?

Solution

It will be noticed that there are two charges being made, the first is a unit charge, the second a standing or fixed charge.

The number of units used is the difference between both sets of reading, i.e.

$$
\begin{array}{r}
59\ 361 \\
-58\ 142 \\
\hline
1\ 219
\end{array}
$$

At the cost of 4.83p/unit

	£
The unit charge is	58.88
Add standing charge	6.37
Total cost	65.25

50 Explain clearly the differences between:
(a) heat and temperature
(b) conduction, convection and radiation
(c) Celsius temperature and kelvin temperature

Solution

(a) *Heat* is a form of energy possessed by a substance, being the product of its mass, its temperature and its specific heat. Heat is transmitted by conduction, convection and radiation and like other forms of energy its unit is the joule or in some cases the kilowatthour.

Temperature is a measure of the intensity of heat energy possessed by a substance, i.e. a measure of its 'hotness'.

A thermometer is an instrument that measures temperature.

(b) *Conduction* is the transmission of heat from places of higher to places of lower temperature in a substance. Heat energy is said to flow through the substance.

Convection is the transference of heat through a liquid or gas by actual movement of the fluid. Portions which are in contact with the source of heat become hotter and expand or rise and their place is taken by colder portions, thus setting up convection currents.

Radiation is the transference of heat in the form of rays, wave motion or particles from a source. Energy is transferred by infra-red rays which can travel through a vacuum at the speed of light. Dull, black surfaces are good radiators and good absorbers while shiny, bright surfaces are poor radiators and poor absorbers.

(c) *Celsius temperature* is centigrade temperature measured on a thermometer scale in which the melting point of ice is 0 °C and the boiling point of water is 100 °C.

Kelvin temperature is the absolute thermodynamic temperature. The kelvin temperature scale has its zero point at 'absolute' zero (i.e. the lowest temperature theoretically possible 0 K). This value is equivalent to −273.15 °C (−273 °C). Celsius boiling point of water is equivalent to 373 K.

Note The difference between the two temperature scales is as follows:

K = °C + 273 and °C = K − 273

Installation theory

Note Questions 51–93 are extracted from *Electrical Installation Technology 1*. Questions 94–100 are additional based on the course syllabus.

51 Write down meanings for the following:
- (a) open circuit
- (b) closed circuit
- (c) short circuit
- (d) polarity
- (e) continuity
- (f) circuit breaker
- (g) insulation resistance
- (h) fusing factor
- (i) current rating
- (j) space factor Ex.2/Q1/Vol.1

Solution

(a) *open circuit* This generally refers to an electrical circuit that has become broken or discontinuous so current cannot flow.

(b) *closed circuit* This generally refers to an electrical circuit that is continuous so that current will flow.

(c) *short circuit* This generally refers to a fault condition whereby live conductors are shorted out.

(d) *polarity* In electrical terms this is an indication of conductor polarity whether it is a 'phase', 'neutral' or 'earth' conductor or whether it is of 'positive' or 'negative' polarity.

(e) *continuity* In electrical terms, this implies a cable's ability to conduct a continuous flow of current through its circuit conductors. Earth continuity

implies an uninterrupted path, preferably of low resistance.

(f) *circuit breaker* A mechanical/electrical device designed to open or close a circuit under normal or abnormal conditions. A miniature moulded case circuit breaker is an example.

(g) *insulation resistance* The insulation medium surrounding and supporting a live or potentially live conductor. Its ohmic value should be very high.

(h) *fusing factor* This is a factor which expresses the minimum fusing current at which a fuse element will melt divided by the current rating.

(i) *current rating* The maximum current that a fuse will carry without exceeding a specified temperature rise.

(j) *space factor* This is a ratio of the sum of the overall cross-sectional areas of cables (including sheath) to the internal cross-sectional area of their enclosure such as conduit and trunking.

52 Write down a meaning for the following terms:
- (a) fuseboard
- (b) consumer unit
- (c) emergency switch
- (d) residual current device
- (e) indirect contact Ex.4/Q1/Vol.1

Solution

(a) *fuseboard* An assemblage of parts, containing one or more fuses or circuit breakers arranged to provide final circuits with excess current protection.

(b) *consumer unit* As in (a) above, but with a main switch incorporated for controlling consumer's final circuits.

(c) *emergency switch* A device for rapidly cutting off the supply of electrical energy.

(d) *residual current device* A mechanical switching device intended to cause the opening of contacts when the device reaches a specific operating condition.

(e) *indirect contact* This means contact of a person (or livestock) with exposed conductive parts that have become live owing to a fault.

53 Draw the following graphical location symbols:
(a) cooker control unit with 13 A socket outlet
(b) twin tube fluorescent luminaire
(c) twin 13 A switched socket outlet
(d) lighting distribution board
(e) main intake point   Ex.4/Q2/Vol.1

Solution

See Figure 18.

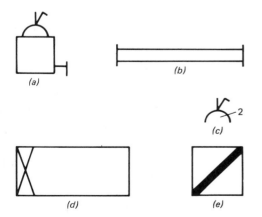

Figure 18

54 Write out in full the following abbreviations of important bodies:
(a) BSI
(b) ECA
(c) JIB
(d) IEE
(e) HSE   Ex.4/Q5/Vol.1

Solution

(a) British Standards Institution
(b) Electrical Contractors' Association
(c) Joint Industry Board
(d) Institution of Electrical Engineers
(e) Health and Safety Executive

Note See pages 22 and 23 of *Electrical Installation Technology 1*.

55 Draw *freehand* the following objects:
(a) HBC fuse
(b) 13 A plug top
(c) brass conduit bush
(d) junior hacksaw
(e) distance saddle   Ex.4/Q6/Vol.1

Solution

See Figure 19.

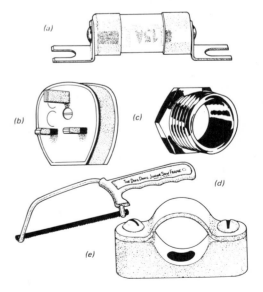

Figure 19

56 Draw separate line diagrams for each of the following final circuits using BS 3939 graphical location symbols:

   (a) one lighting point controlled by two-way intermediate switching

   (b) one immersion heater controlled by a double-pole switch

   (c) one 13 A socket outlet ring circuit comprising six sockets on the ring and three spurs at different points on the ring supplying socket outlets

   (d) one cooker control point controlling a cooking appliance

   (e) two fluorescent luminaires (both twin tubes) controlled by two-way switching

Ex.4/Q10/Vol.1

Solution

See Figure 20.

57 Figure 21(a) shows the rooms in a three-bedroom house. Insert in each room the appropriate BS 3939 installation graphical symbols for lighting and power. Use colour pencils to distinguish between lighting and power. See the example symbols given in bedroom 3.

Ex.5/Q1/Vol.1

Solution

See Figure 21(b) on page 34.

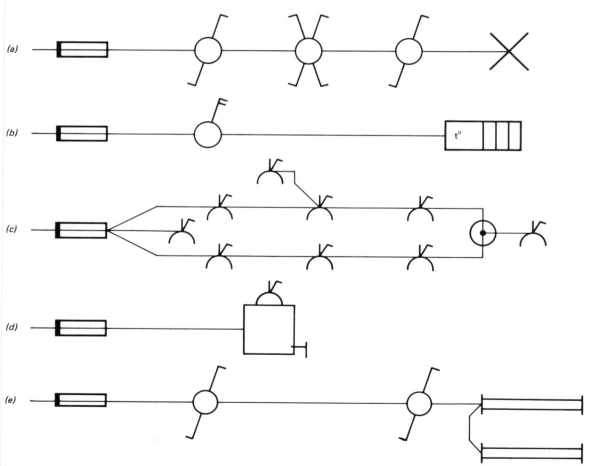

Figure 20

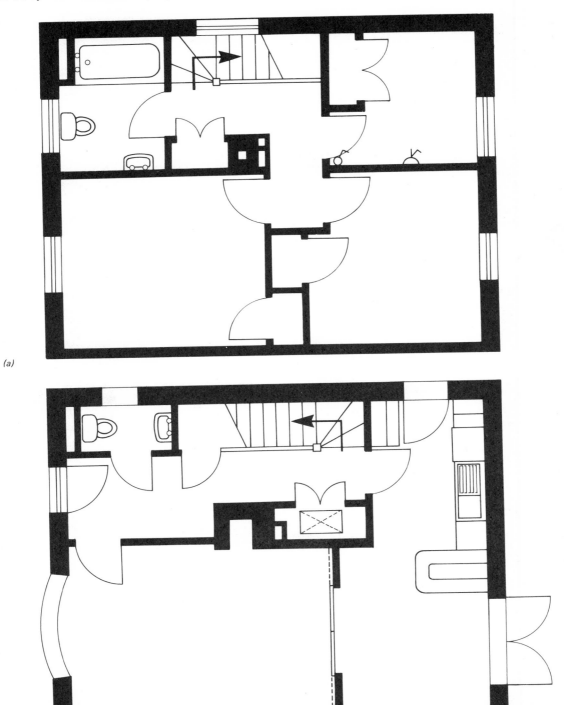

(a)

Figure 21 (a)

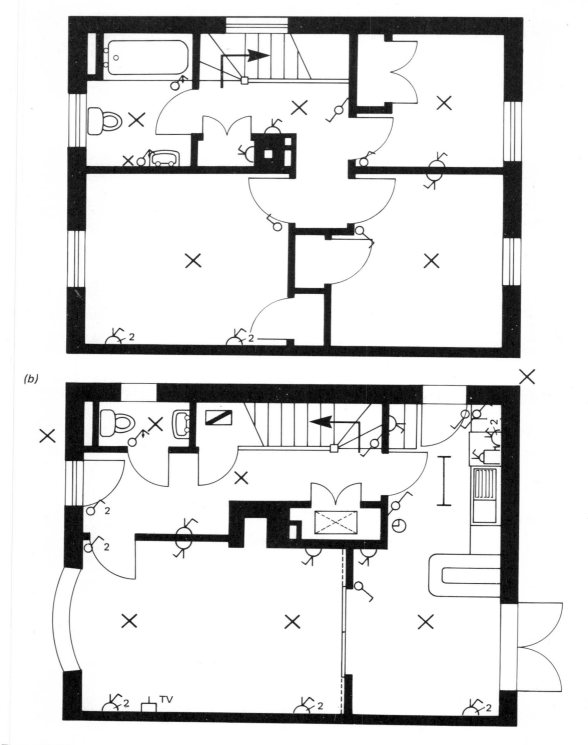

(b)

Figure 21 (b)

58 Explain the procedure you would take in attempting to rescue a fellow workmate who was receiving an electric shock whilst holding a portable drill.   Ex.6/Q1/Vol.1

Solution

Some guidance notes on electric shock treatment are to be found on pages 36–8, *Electrical Installation Technology 1*. One's first reaction is to immediately switch off the electrical supply. Since the tool is a portable drill its lead will not be very long and should easily be traced to a supply source. Where this may not be the case, your workmate has to be released from contact with the drill using some form of non-conducting material, such as rubber gloves, dry clothing, dry wood or a length of PVC tubing.

If your workmate is in an unconscious state and not breathing (looking pale or even blue if the airway is blocked), start mouth-to-mouth first aid treatment. Only a few seconds delay can mean the difference between success and failure. The procedure is given below supported by Figure 22:

(a) Kneel by your workmate's head and quickly inspect the mouth for any obstructions. Loosen clothing around the neck.

(b) Move the patient's head fully back (as shown), breathe in deeply, seal your lips over his or hers, pinch the nostrils with one hand and breathe out into the body.

(c) Watch the patient's chest rise and then turn your head away and breathe in once more. Repeat the procedure about ten to twelve times every minute and continue until he or she is breathing satisfactorily or until you are told by a doctor to stop.

(d) If your workmate recovers before the doctor arrives (someone should have been sent to get help), keep him or her warm and place in a recovery position.

A further stage in the treatment of electric shock is described in *Electrical Installation Technology 2*, but carrying out this method (external heart compression) requires first-aid training.

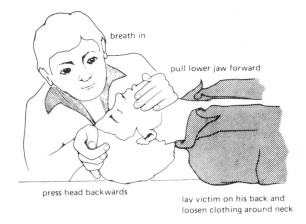

breath in

pull lower jaw forward

press head backwards

lay victim on his back and loosen clothing around neck

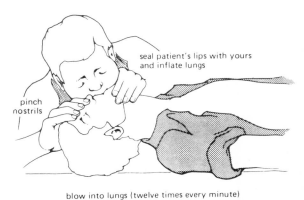

seal patient's lips with yours and inflate lungs

pinch nostrils

blow into lungs (twelve times every minute) avoid patient's exhaled air

Figure 22

59 Explain the operation of a residual current device.   Ex.6/Q2/Vol.1

Solution

The device is described on page 95 of *Electrical Installation Technology 1* and illustrated in Figure 23. It will be seen that both live conductors, i.e. phase and neutral conductors, pass around a toroidal transformer core before connection is made to the load circuit. Both windings have an equal and opposite number of turns so that no flux will be induced in the core to set up a circulating trip current through the detector coil circuit. This will only be the

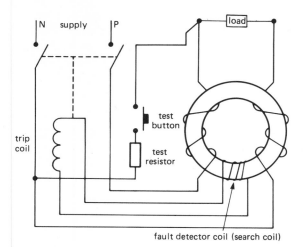

Figure 23

case when the device detects no earth fault. A short circuit between phase and neutral would also not cause the device to trip out since its operation has to detect an imbalance in the phase and neutral currents on each side of the core. Any leakage to earth on the load side in one of the live conductors, allows the ampere-turns (induced flux) to be greater in the other conductor and circulate a flux around the core. Notice that the detector coil and trip coil form a closed circuit (see the solution to Question 51(b)). Also notice how the test circuit is wired between phase and neutral.

60   What tests would you make on an electrical appliance to find out if it was safe to use?

Ex.6/Q3/Vol.1

Solution

The first check that one should do is a visual inspection of the lead and entry of it into the appliance and plug top (or supply source if the appliance is fixed). The inspection of the lead will reveal any wear on the outer sheath, while at entry points one can look for loose cable grips and attachments. Inspection within the plug top and appliance will reveal correct polarity of the flexible lead conductor cores. Look for unnecessary stress on conductors, identification tags (if any), loose termination

screws, secure earthing if the appliance is not double insulated. Check size of lead against the rating of the appliance to see if it will adequately carry the load current. Check fuse size and see if any cover screws are missing; also check safety guards (if any).

The appliance needs to be tested for insulation resistance between conductors (phase and neutral) and these conductors and earth. This test uses an instrument called an *ohmmeter* and the readings obtained must be in excess of 0.5 megohms. Before this test is applied, however, a test of protective conductor continuity is made, and here, the d.c. ohmmeter may be used — see item 3, Appendix 15, IEE Regulations. For further reference, see the description on page 99 and Figure 123, in *Electrical Installation Technology 1*.

61   Describe how you would fix a large metal busbar chamber to a brick wall using rawlbolts.

Ex.6/Q4/Vol.1

Solution

A typical large busbar chamber is one of 500 A rating and measuring some 527 × 1 384 × 175 mm (HWD). It will have switchgear and fusegear mounted above and below it and room must be allowed for these items of apparatus. Having established its correct height, the busbar chamber is offered up to the wall and marked accordingly using a spirit level to obtain horizontal and vertical alignment. Also, check the wall markings against the brickwork line.

The two most common methods of drilling the wall to fix rawlbolts are (a) using a stardrill and (b) using a tipped masonry drill. The latter method is preferred and includes the use of a hammer drill and rotary impact drilling machine. Whatever method is used, eye protection should be worn. The correct drill bit must be chosen for the rawlbolt size outer diameter and often bolt projecting rawlbolts are chosen for this purpose. The base of these bolts is shaped to form an expander wedge and when the nut is tightened against the outer fixing, the expander wedge is drawn through the rawlbolt shell to provide a very tight fixing.

Only the thread of the rawlbolt should be showing for each hole and the busbar chamber mounted on these and erected in position, applying the nut and washer to secure the fixing of each rawlbolt.

62 In relation to Question 58, complete the accident form found on page 36 of *Electrical Installation Technology 1* using fictitious names and addresses. Ex.6/Q5/Vol.1

Solution

See Figure 24.

NOTICE OF ACCIDENT OR DANGEROUS OCCURRENCE

1. **OCCUPIER OF PREMISES**
Name J.A. TOWNSHOTT LTD
Address 5 APPLEBY WAY, ELY
Nature of Business BRICKWORKS

2. **EMPLOYER OF INJURED PERSON** (if different from above)
Name
Address

3. **INJURED PERSON**
Surname SPARK
Christian Names IAN
Resident/~~Staff~~
Widow/~~Widower~~
Married/~~Single~~
Date of Birth 6.7.38 Occupation ELEC-TRICIAN
Address 12 OAK LANE, WOOTEN
Name and address of parent or guardian
Mr & Mrs J.A. SPARK
108 ELM DRIVE, WOOTEN

4. **PLACE WHERE INCIDENT OCCURRED**
Address 5 APPLEBY WAY, ELY
Exact Location (e.g. staircase to office, canteen storeroom, classroom
STOREROOM
Name of Person supervising J. FLASH

5. **INJURIES AND DISABLEMENT**
Fatal or non Fatal NON FATAL
Nature and extent of injury (e.g. fracture of leg, laceration of arm, scalded foot, scratch on hand followed by sepsis)
ELECTRIC SHOCK FROM FAULTY PORTABLE DRILL

6. **ACCIDENT OR DANGEROUS OCCURRENCE**
Date 13th JULY 1983   Time 11.00 A.M.
Full details of how the incident occurred and what the injured person was doing. If a fall of person or materials, plant, etc. state height of fall.

MR SPARK WAS DRILLING A METAL BOX AT THE TIME OF THE ACCIDENT.

Name and address of any witness.
MR. P. BROWN,
22 WINDSOR ROAD, LILLY, KENT.

If due to machinery, state name and type of machine
What part of the machine caused the accident?
Was the machine in motion by mechanical power at the time?

7. **ACTION FOLLOWING THE ACCIDENT**
What happened? MR SPARK WAS TREATED FOR ELECTRIC SHOCK
When was the doctor informed? 11.00 A.M.
When did he attend? 11.15 A.M.
Name of Doctor P.G. BONE (address and telephone) BROMHAM LANE SURGERY BROM 61062
If taken to hospital, say when and where 11.45 A.M. TO UPTON HOSPITAL.
Names and addresses of friends or relatives who have been notified of the accident:
PARENTS (SEE ABOVE)
When and how were they informed? 11.45 A.M. TELEPHONE

Signature of injured person or person completing this form:
J. Flash   Date: 13/7/83
If the form is completed by some person acting on the injured person's behalf, the address and occupation of such person should be entered.

Figure 24

63 Make a sketch of a 13 A plug top, fully label its internal connections and parts. Describe how you would terminate a flex into the plug top.
Ex.6/Q6/Vol.1

Solution

A sketch of the plug top is shown in Figure 25 with the essential parts labelled. A description on wiring the plug top is given on page 35 of *Electrical Installation Technology 1*. Essential points to note are:

(a) only strip sufficient insulation away from internal conductors

(b) anchor strands on terminals in a clock-wise direction and do not screw terminal over the insulation. Check polarity

(c) insert flex in the wedge cable grip before fitting plug cover

(d) remember to check the fuse size for the equipment being used

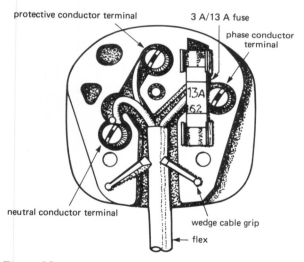

Figure 25

64 A two-way lighting circuit has become faulty due to a recent alteration in the switch position-ing. Describe the precautions taken in rectifying the fault and mention the possible troubles with the circuit wiring.
Ex.6/Q7/Vol.1

Solution

If only one switch has been altered then it is quite obvious that the trouble will be here.

However, keep an open mind in case it so happens that a fault has developed elsewhere. First, switch off the circuit supply or remove the lighting fuse, whichever is convenient. Since the question does not indicate what kind of fault exists let us assume it is one where the light sometimes doesn't work from one switch-ing position and only works in one direction from the other switching position. The cause of the fault here will be that the live feed has been inserted in one of the strapper wire terminals. If the light does not work at all, it is possible that the conductor feed or switch wire has broken off inside its terminal. If the fault cannot be traced visually by inspection at the altered switch position and the fault is one of no light, check the lamp itself and the fuse — although the fuse rupturing would have meant other circuits having trouble. Where the fault causes the fuse to rupture, then it is likely to be an earth fault in the switch. Check wiring polarity and earth sleeving. See Figure 26 for possible cause.

65 Why is it sometimes necessary to earth the metal cover of a 13 A socket outlet to its box? What size protective conductor is normally used for this purpose?
Ex.6/Q8/Vol.1

Solution

In practice, where metal conduit is used to provide the protective conductor of a wiring system, then socket outlet boxes attached to the conduit must provide good earth con-tinuity. The metal cover plate of these boxes is held fast by two fixing screws which are inadequate as a means of providing continuity with the rest of the box, particularly if the mounting box is for flush wiring having an adjustable lug (see Figure 27). It is a require-ment of the IEE Wiring Regulations, Reg. 543—10 that a separate protective conductor must connect the box to the socket outlet via an earthing terminal incorporated within the box. The minimum size protective conductor is 2.5 mm². See IEE Wiring Regulations, Reg. 547—4.

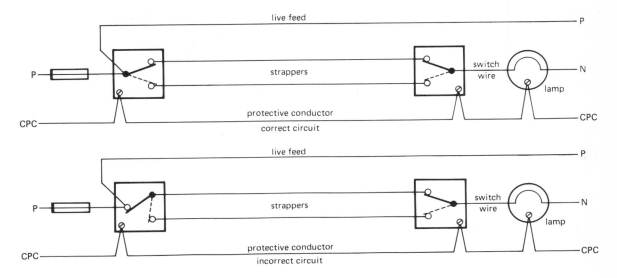

Figure 26

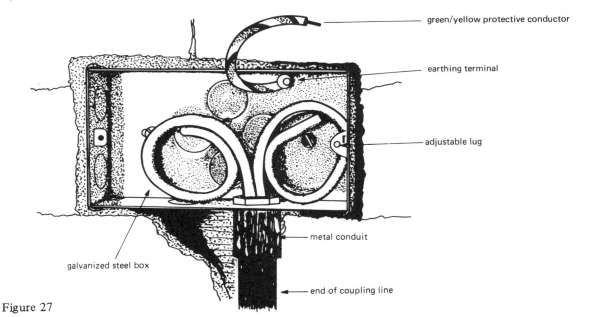

Figure 27

66 What is the difference between a PME system (TN–C–S system) and an SNE system (TN–S system)? Try to explain with the aid of diagrams. Ex.6/Q9/Vol.1

Solution

The abbreviation PME means *protective multiple earthing* whereas SNE means *separate neutral and protective conductors*. In the former case, the method is commonly used where the source of energy incorporates multiple earthing of the neutral — the letter *C* in TN–C–S means that the neutral and protective conductors are common in a single conductor called a *PEN* conductor or combined neutral earth conductor (CNE). The PEN conductor is only taken as far as a consumer's supply terminals and from this point on in the premises, separate neutral and earth conductors are taken. The letter *S* in TN–C–S indicates this.

With regard to the SNE system, this system involves both a separate neutral and separate protective conductor run from the supply source to separate terminals at each consumer's premises. In practice, the supply cable sheath/armouring provides the protective function and the neutral conductor is incorporated in the cable along with the phase conductors. Figure

28 shows both these systems. Notice the earthing conductor connections.

67 Make a neat circuit diagram of a 110 V electric drill fed by a double wound transformer with its primary winding connected to a 240 V single phase supply. Show earthing of the transformer and electric drill.

Ex.6/Q10/Vol.1

Solution

See Figure 29.

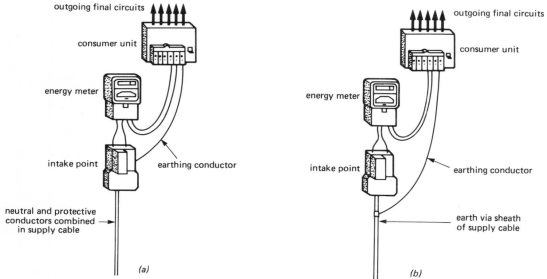

Figure 28   (a) *TNC–S system*
            (b) *TNS system*

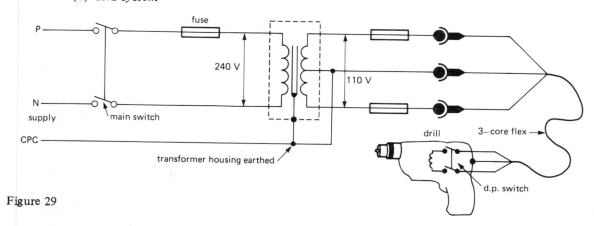

Figure 29

68 A 15 kW heating load is to be installed 10 m away from a 240 V distribution board using PVC insulated single core copper cables in plastic conduit. Circuit protection in the distribution board is by BS 1361 fuses and the installation is in an ambient temperature of 35 °C. Select a suitable size cable for the load, working through the following steps:

(a) calculate the design current of the circuit

(b) make reference to the IEE Wiring Regulations, Table 9A, type A, and also Table D1, to ascertain the ambient temperature correction factor

(c) note there is no correction factor for BS 1361 fuses

(d) find from Table 41A2(b) the nearest fuse size to design current

(e) divide the correction factor into the fuse size

(f) select a cable from Table 9D1

(g) check the volt drop (see IEE Wiring Regulations, Reg. 522–8

Ex.8/Q1/Vol.1

Solution

(a) $I_B = \dfrac{P}{V} = \dfrac{15\,000}{240} = \textbf{62.5 A}$

(b) Table 9A, enclosure type A is on page 145 of the IEE Wiring Regulations (red book)

(c) Proceed as instructed in item 4(i) IEE Wiring Regulations

(d) Nearest size fuse to design current of 62.5 A is **80 A**

(e) From Table 9D1 ambient temperature correction factors, choose 0.94. The current carrying capacity of the selected cable must be not less than:

$$\dfrac{\text{nominal circuit rating of protective device}}{\text{correction factors}}$$

thus: $I_Z = \dfrac{80}{0.94} = \textbf{85.1 A}$

(f) From column 2 of Table 9D1, 25 mm² has a current carrying capacity of 97 A with a cable voltage drop 1.7 mV per ampere per metre.

(g) Checking its volt drop against the permissible 2.5% of the declared voltage (240 V × 2.5/100 = 6 V), then:

$$V = \dfrac{\text{length of run} \times \text{design current}}{1000} \times mV$$

$$= \dfrac{10 \times 62.5 \times 1.7}{1000}$$

$$= \textbf{1.06 V}$$

This cable is satisfactory from both the temperature point of view and volt drop permitted.

69 In Question 68 above, assume the heating load circuit is protected by a semi-enclosed fuse to BS 3036 and, instead of PVC cables in plastic conduit, the cable chosen for the circuit is a twin armoured PVC insulated copper cable. From Table 9D3 of the IEE Wiring Regulations, select an appropriate cable size. The conditions remain as before except that in this case the cable will be clipped direct to the surface. Working through the following steps:

(a) refer to Table 9D3

(b) refer to Appendix 9, item 4(ii) and carry out the calculations. *Note* Refer to Table 41A2(c) and divide by the correction factors.

(c) determine the cable size from Table 9D3

(d) check the volt drop   Ex.8/Q2/Vol.1

Solution

(a) This Table is on page 152 of the IEE Wiring Regulations (red book).

(b) Using Appendix 9, page 144, the calculation is as follows:

$I_B = \textbf{62.5 A}$ (design current)

Nearest fuse (nominal current) is **100 A** (see Table 41A2(c))

Read Note at foot of Table 9D3 and use correction factor given on page 144, i.e. 35 °C amb. temp. is 0.97

Also note the use of 0.725 correction factor because a semi-enclosed fuse has a fusing factor of approx. 2 (see IEE Wiring Regulations, Reg. 433–2), then

$$I_Z = \dfrac{100}{0.97 \times 0.725} = \textbf{142.2 A}$$

(c)   Nearest cable size from column 2, Table 9D3 is 35 mm² having a current carrying capacity of 142 A and millivolt drop/ampere/metre of 1.8 mV

(d)   Checking volt drop:

$$V = \frac{10 \times 62.5 \times 1.8}{1000} = 1.12 \text{ V}$$

This cable satisfies both temperature and type of excess current protection as well as volt drop conditions.

70   Make a sketch of a shell type transformer, showing the primary and secondary windings connected to the centre limb of the core.

Ex.9/Q4/Vol.1

Solution

See Figure 30.

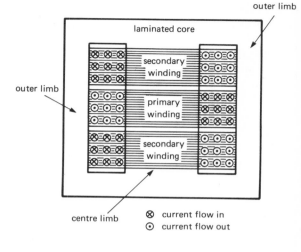

Figure 30   *Shell transformer showing sandwiched primary and secondary windings*

71   Draw the single-pole switching arrangements for two-way and intermediate control of a lamp. Label all conductors in the circuit.

Ex.10/Q1/Vol.1

Solution

See Figure 31.

72   Draw a circuit diagram of a 13 A radial circuit feeding six socket outlets. If the circuit covers an area greater than 30 m² and it is wired in MIMS cable, indicate on the drawing the size of the conductors used and the main final circuit fuse.

Ex.10/Q2/Vol.1

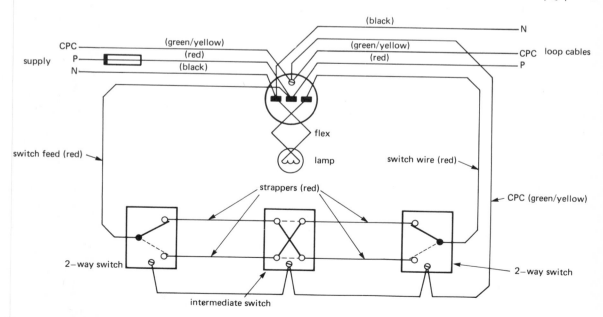

Figure 31   *Two-way and intermediate switching*

Solution

See Figure 32.

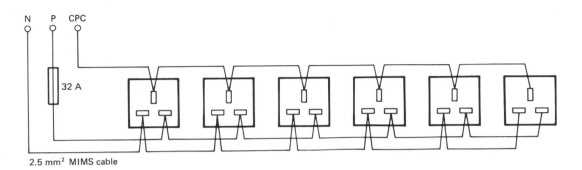

Figure 32

---

73 Where on a ring circuit is it possible to wire and connect non-fused spurs? How many socket outlets (13 A) can be fed by non-fused spurs?

Ex.10/Q3/Vol.1

Solution

Reference should be made to the IEE Wiring Regulations, page 114, Appendix 5. Briefly, from the point of view of BS 1363 socket outlets, a non-fused spur feeds only one single or one twin socket outlet or one permanently connected piece of equipment and must be connected at a socket outlet on the ring or at a joint box, or it may be connected from the fuse position in the distribution board which supplies the ring circuit — this is called the origin of the circuit.

The number of non-fused spurs must not exceed the total number of socket outlets and stationary equipment connected within the ring circuit.

In final circuits using BS 196 socket outlets, non-fused spurs are not used.

74 Explain how an immersion heater thermostat operates.

Ex.10/Q4/Vol.1

Solution

First, a thermostat is a temperature-sensing control that operates by cycling during normal use and which is designed to keep the temperature of an appliance between certain values. Immersion heater thermostats are generally designed to the specifications of BS 3955 and the tests prescribed therein to see if they have insufficient self-heat to cycle when their temperature-sensing elements are maintained at any suitable constant temperature.

The type often used for controlling temperature of domestic water heaters is made of brass and operates a single-pole micro-gap switch. Figure 33 illustrates this type of thermostat, where it will be seen that the brass tube and invar steel rod (non-expanding rod) are joined at one end. This is done so that when the temperature rises in the heated water, the expansion of the brass tube reduces the pressure on the pressure block and the contacts separate. The small magnet allows the mechanism to have a snap action effect to avoid unnecessary sparking and radio interference. The temperature scale and adjusting knob are fitted in the head of a moulded plastic cover. It should be pointed out that in hard water areas, the thermostat setting should not be higher than 60–65 °C.

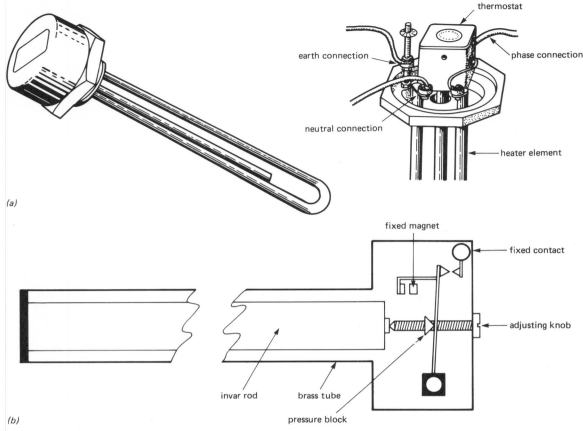

Figure 33   (a) *Immersion heater*
             (b) *Water heater thermostat*

75   Draw a circuit diagram of a residual current device and explain how it operates. What are the IEE Wiring Regulations requirements regarding the testing of e.l.c.b.s?

Ex.10/Q5/Vol.1

Solution

A residual current device has already been described in Question 59 and shown in Figure 23. With regard to testing the devices, reference should be made to the IEE Wiring Regulations, Reg. 613–16 and Item 6 of Appendix 15.

The type shown in Figure 23 is called 'passive' since it does not require electronic amplification of its operating current. The value required to protect users against indirect contact is 30 mA. The test in Item 6 is shown in Figure 134 of *Electrical Installation Tech-*

nology 1, page 108. It will be seen that the secondary voltage (max. 50 V a.c.) is applied across the neutral and earth conductors of the socket outlet and the residual device should operate instantly. It should be pointed out that the device cannot be used in a TN–C installation since there are no separate neutral and earth conductors to cause an imbalance to trip the device out.

76   Redraw the ring final circuit of Figure 79 in *Electrical Installation Technology 1* and incorporate 13 A socket outlets at:
(a)   the origin of the circuit
(b)   a socket outlet on the ring
(c)   a joint box half-way round the ring

Ex.10/Q7/Vol.1

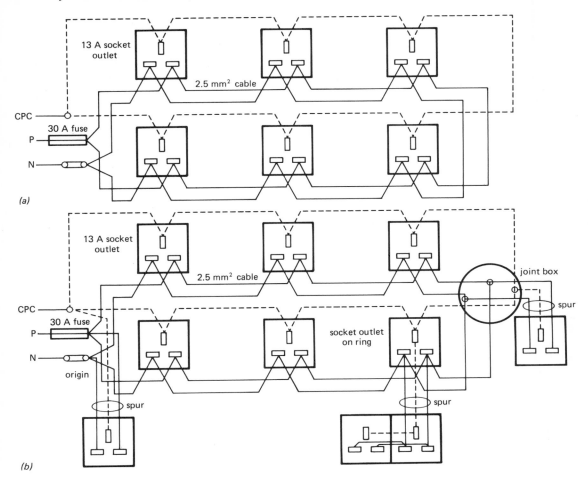

Figure 34

Solution

This question could have been incorporated in Question 73, however, the solution is shown in Figure 34.

77 Explain the use of the following circuit components:
   (a) power factor correction capacitor
   (b) choke
   (c) current transformer
   (d) voltage transformer
   (e) contactor

Ex.10/Q8/Vol.1

Solution

(a) A *power factor correction capacitor* is a component which neutralizes the effect created by an inductive circuit component, such as a choke, transformer winding or motor field winding, when the components are connected to an a.c. supply. These components tend to have lagging power factors whereas the capacitor component has a leading power factor.

(b) A *choke* is an inductive component used to operate a discharge lamp; it may sometimes be called a *ballast*. In a fluorescent tube circuit, the choke provides the initial voltage surge to strike an arc across the lamp electrodes. Once this occurs the choke then protects the circuit by limiting the amount of current through the lamp.

(c) A *current transformer* is an instrument transformer used for measurement whereby, for example, an ammeter, usually designed to give a full scale deflection of 5 A, can in fact be used with the transformer to read a small proportion of a large load current. The current transformer allows the use of much smaller cross-sectional area conductors for measurement purposes.

(d) A *voltage transformer* is again an instrument transformer used for measuring low voltage from high voltage installations; they make it possible to use standard low voltage cables for measurement since their measuring voltage is usually at 110 V.

(e) A *contactor* is a power control device comprising a magnetic core, operating coil and associated contacts. It is used for the automatic opening and closing of circuits.

78   Draw a circuit diagram of a block storage radiator. How is it able to retain its heat when the supply is switched off?

Ex.10/Q9/Vol.1

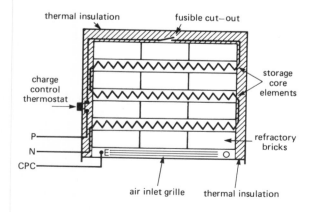

Figure 35

Solution

See Figure 35. The storage radiator is able to retain its heat because of the very good thermal conductivity of its refractory bricks and thermal insulation such as mineral wool and glass fibre lining the inside casing of the heater. The heater will normally be operating between the hours of 1.0 a.m. and 7.0 a.m. to store its heat.

79   Describe the internal layout of a metalclad, six-way consumer unit fitted with m.c.b.s.

Ex.10/Q10/Vol.1

Solution

A metalclad consumer unit is a factory-built assembly (see 'Definitions', in IEE Wiring Regulations, page 9) and for indoor use, designed to the specification of BS 5486, Part 13 (1979). The two main features of the consumer unit will be miniature circuit breakers and main switch which often takes the form of a double-pole earth leakage circuit breaker of the residual current type (i.e. RCD), rated between 30 A and 100 A.

The miniature circuit breakers are to BS 3871 specification and come in current ratings of 5 A, 10 A, 15 A, 20 A, 30 A, 40 A, 45 A and 50 A. These devices are arranged in line with each other with a common busbar linking the lower m.c.b. terminals and the outgoing phase connection of the RCD. The RCD also has an outgoing multi-terminal neutral and the device provides protection against current leakage to earth with tripping values commonly at 30 mA, 100 mA and 300 mA.

The interior assembly is often mounted on a removable sub-plate to allow the consumer unit to be fixed in position. The consumer unit enclosure will have a conveniently positioned earth bar and ample knockout entry holes for final circuit wiring. All units will be provided with circuit identification labels and instruction information. It is important, when wiring inside the unit, to terminate the conductors correctly, making sure that circuit earth and neutral conductors follow the same wiring order as the phase conductor into its respective m.c.b.

80 Describe the advantages and disadvantages of the following systems:
- (a) catenary wiring
- (b) earth concentric wiring
- (c) pre-fabricated wiring
- (d) flexible conduit
- (e) underfloor duct system

Ex.11/Q1/Vol.1

Solution

(a) This system is often used as an alternative to burying a wiring system in the ground which could prove costly. It is ideal for temporary supplies and supplies needed for out-buildings as found in agricultural and horticultural installations. The wire used is galvanized steel wire which is strained tight. From this the wiring system cable, e.g. rubber or PVC sheathed cable, is taped or suspended by hangers. Some systems have integral cable and catenary wire. The IEE Regulations restrict the height of aerial cables incorporating catenary wire to 3.5 m above ground where vehicles are inaccessible and 5.2 m where they are accessible apart from road crossings where the minimum height is 5.8 m. It should be noted that the 3.5 m height mentioned is not applicable to agricultural premises.

In terms of disadvantages, the catenary wiring system is restricted in use and has not the flexibility of use of other wiring systems found today, such as conduit and trunking systems where circuits can be easily altered. The catenary system does not provide a high degree of mechanical protection.

(b) In this system, the immediate advantage is found by the sheath being used as a return conductor. Basically, the wiring system used is MIMS cable since its outer sheath is copper, which provides an ideal PEN conductor. Sealing pots which contain an earthing tail are used for this purpose. While the system has the advantage of not requiring any neutral conductors contained within the cable itself, its use as a wiring system is some-what restricted to installations not connected directly to the public supply. Furthermore, where MIMS is used as the wiring system, the sheath must not have a c.s.a. of less than 4 mm^2 and its resistance must never be more than any of its internal conductors. Other conditions for its use are given in the IEE Wiring Regulations, Regs. 546–1 to 546–8.

(c) This system has the advantages of reduced cost of site installation time since it is prepared off-site. It is often supplied pre-wired, depending on the type of system, with cables cut to length ready for termination. In practice, the system lends itself to duplicate installations, such as domestic dwellings and it is important that manufacturers site information is adhered to during installation. Multi-bore and Octoflex are typical systems used today.

The disadvantages of the prefabricated systems are their restrictions in general use, flexibility of installation practice and site alterations.

(d) Flexible conduit systems have a somewhat restricted use as a wiring system, their main advantage being where electrical equipment and apparatus requires moving or is vibrating such as the wiring to a motor. The system should preferably be waterproof and if of metallic design its enclosure should not be relied upon as a protective conductor.

(e) This system has particular use in commercial premises particularly large office blocks with requirements for numerous business machines, electric typewriters, duplicators, photocopiers etc., spread about the building. While the system has numerous advantages in the premises described, it is again somewhat restricted, since, once installed it cannot be modified without a great deal of expense and inconvenience. Careful planning at the design stages of the building are essential as well as at the installation stage to avoid damage to the system before it is covered *in situ*.

81 What are the special requirements in the IEE Wiring Regulations for (a) flexible cables and flexible cords, and (b) heating wires and cables?
Ex.11/Q2/Vol.1

Solution

(a) Flexible cables and cords are dealt with in Chapter 52 of the IEE Regulations (see Tables 9H2 and 9H3). Generally speaking, flexible cables have sizes ranging from 4.0 mm² to 630 mm², whereas flexible cords range from 0.5 mm² to 4.0 mm².

While Regulation 521–5 (concerning the cables used at low voltage) provides examples of the types of cable, it does not concern itself with flexible cords forming part of portable appliances or luminaires or to those cables for combined power and telecommunications wiring, these latter cables being the subject of Regulation 525–8. This regulation is one of twelve requirements concerned with prevention of mutual detrimental influence. Briefly, circuits are split up into categories of circuits, C1 being a circuit operating at low voltage fed from a mains supply system (it excludes a fire alarm circuit or emergency lighting circuit), C2 being any circuit for telecommunications, such as radio, intruder alarm, data system etc. (it again excludes a fire alarm and emergency lighting circuit), and C3 being a fire alarm circuit and emergency lighting circuit.

It is Regulation 525–8 which relates to the way the flexible cables and flexible cords should be used with each other or separated from each other as the case may be in terms of their category identification. Figure 36 illustrates this arrangement of segregation of circuits.

(b) These regulations are dealt with in Chapter 55 of the IEE Wiring Regulations under the sub-heading: 'Conductors and cables for soil, road and floor warming'. Regulation 554–31 requires cables to be enclosed in material having class P ignitability characteristics, specified in BS 467: Part 5. They should also

partitioned metal trunking containing all three category circuits

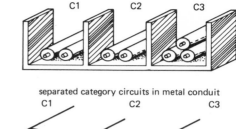

separated category circuits in metal conduit

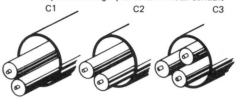

common enclosure for C1 and C2 circuits provided C2 circuits are insulated to same standard as C1 circuits

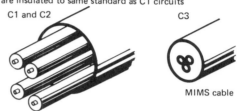

MIMS cable

Figure 36

be protected from mechanical damage (see Reg. 554–32) and be constructed of materials that are resistant to damage from dampness and/or corrosion. In Regulation 554–33 the concern for heating cables laid below surfaces is that they should be completely embedded in the substance they intend to heat as well as not suffer damage by any natural movement they may have or from the substance which surrounds them. Reference should be made to Table 55D with regard to maximum operating temperatures for floor warming cables (see also Reg. 554–34).

82 What are the IEE Wiring Regulations concerning:
(a) space factor for cables drawn into ducts
(b) single-core, PVC cables drawn through metal conduit

(c) cables unsuitable for a.c.

(d) maximum operating temperature of PVC compound cables contained within luminaires   Ex.11/Q3/Vol.1

Solution

(a) Regulation 529–7 points out that the number of cables laid in the enclosure of a wiring system shall be such that no damage is caused to the cables or its enclosure. The IEE Regulations provide no data on percentage limitations and one should seek information from duct manufacturers.

(b) The requirement for single-core cables is spelt out in Reg. 521–8, and the enclosure of metal conduit around a single-core conductor creates eddy currents (see Figure 37) which cause the conduit to become hot.

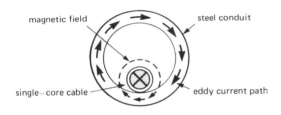

Figure 37

(c) See Reg. 521–8 again – the reason is given in (b) above.

(d) See section 523, IEE Wiring Regulations, 'ambient temperature'. Also see Table 9D1, 9D2 and 9D3 conductor operating temperature 70 °C.

Note Heat resisting flexible cords are recommended between a ceiling rose and lampholder such as silicone rubber or glass-fibre, particularly in luminaires using tungsten lamps.

83 Make a neat sketch showing how solid conduit elbows and tees can be used, complying with Regulation 529–4 of the IEE Wiring Regulations.   Ex.11/Q4/Vol.1

Solution

See Figure 38.

84 With reference to Appendix 12 of the IEE Wiring Regulations, calculate suitable trunking sizes for the following installed cables:

(a) nine 10 mm² single-core PVC insulated cables, each having an overall diameter of 6.2 mm

(b) four 16 mm² single-core PVC insulated cables, each having an overall diameter of 7.3 mm   Ex.11/Q5/Vol.1

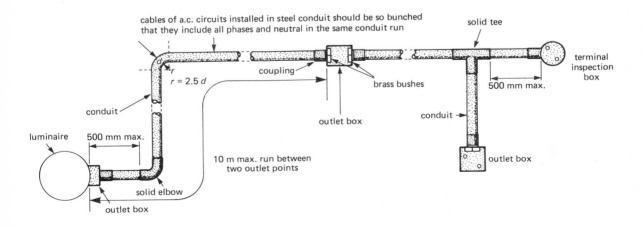

Figure 38

Solution

(a) First, find the c.s.a. of one 10 mm²
cable, using:

$$A = \frac{\pi \times d^2}{4}$$

$$= \frac{3.142 \times 6.2 \times 6.2}{4}$$

$$= \frac{120.778}{4}$$

$$= 30.19 \text{ mm}^2$$

The overall c.s.a. of the cables is 9 ×
30.19 = 271.71 mm²

Make reference to Appendix 12 of
the IEE Wiring Regulations, Table 12E.
If the factor of 36.3 was chosen for each
10 mm² then the overall c.s.a. would be
9 × 36.3 = **326.7 mm²**.

However, since specific information is
given in the question, then a suitable
trunking size from Table 12F is 75 mm ×
25 mm having a factor of 738 which
satisfies both calculations.

(b) The overall c.s.a. of this cable is:

$$A = \frac{\pi \times d^2}{4}$$

$$= \frac{3.142 \times 7.3 \times 7.3}{4}$$

$$= 41.86 \text{ mm}^2$$

For four cables it is 4 × 41.86 =
167.44 mm²
From the note at the foot of the Tables,
use has to be made of the space factor
of 45%. Thus:

$$A = 167.44 \times \frac{100}{45} = \textbf{372 mm}^2$$

Again the 75 mm × 25 mm trunking will
be found suitable.

85 Draw a circuit diagram of a fault-voltage
operated protective device being tested in
compliance with Regulation 613–16, IEE
Wiring Regulations.   Ex.12/Q1/Vol.1

Solution

See Figure 39 and also Figure 19, Appendix
15 of the IEE Wiring Regulations.

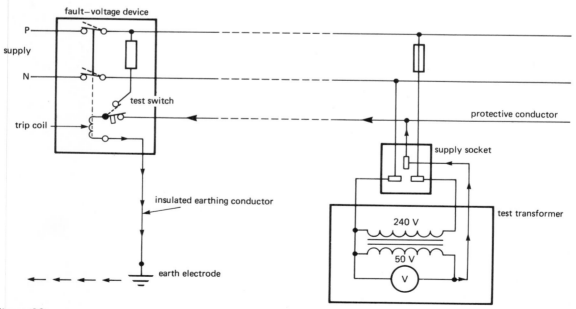

Figure 39

86 Draw diagrams to illustrate the following methods of protection:
- (a) protection by barriers or enclosures
- (b) protection by placing out of reach
- (c) protection by obstacles
- (d) protection by insulation of live parts

Ex.12/Q3/Vol.1

Solution

See Figure 40.

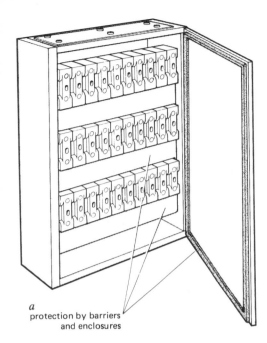

a
protection by barriers and enclosures

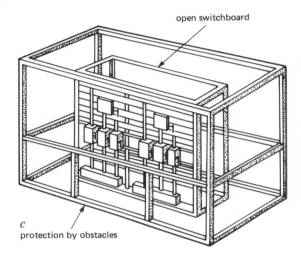

c
protection by obstacles

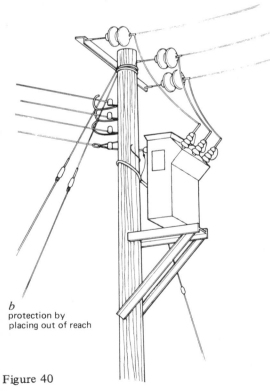

b
protection by placing out of reach

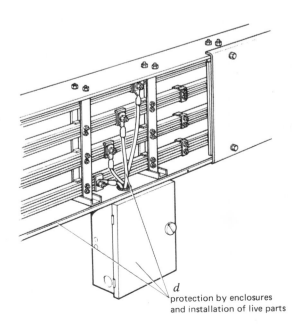

d
protection by enclosures and installation of live parts

Figure 40

87   Explain the following:
     (a)   earth fault loop impedance
     (b)   earth electrode resistance
     (c)   prospective short circuit
     (d)   inspection certificate
     (e)   extraneous conductive part

                                        Ex.12/Q2/Vol.1

Solution

(a)   For a phase to earth fault, it is the im-
      pedance of the circuit starting and ending
      at the point of earth fault.

(b)   The resistance of a conductor or group
      of conductors in intimate contact with
      and providing an electrical connection to
      earth.

(c)   This is a term given to current which is
      possible to flow under extreme short
      circuit conditions.

(d)   This is a certificate given by an electrical
      contractor or other person responsible
      for carrying out inspection and testing of
      an electrical installation.

(e)   This term refers to a conductive part
      which does not form part of the electrical
      installation.

Note See 'Definitions' in the IEE Wiring Regulations,
pages 7–12.

88   What are some of the requirements of the IEE
     Wiring Regulations with regard to measurement
     of earth electrode resistance?

                                        Ex.12/Q4/Vol.1

Solution

Item 4 of Appendix 15 covers the measurement
of earth electrode resistance. Briefly, a test of

earth electrode resistance involves the use of
either a hand-driven generator tester or mains
supply transformer. The former incorporates a
rectifier and direct reading ohmmeter while the
latter includes a variable resistor to adjust the
test current. For tests made at supply frequency,
the requirements state that the source of supply
must be isolated, hence the use of a double-
wound transformer. Also, the electrode under
test must be disconnected from its normal
earthing conductor. The voltmeter used in this
test must have a resistance value in the order of
200 ohms/volt. If not, its resistance will be in
parallel with the earth electrode resistance and
produce a false voltage reading.

The test requires the average of three readings
to be taken where the second auxiliary electrode
is moved 6 m closer to the test electrode and
then 6 m further away from the test electrode.
If there is no substantial agreement between the
readings then the first auxiliary electrode must
be moved further away from the test electrode.
The important thing is that these two electrode
resistance areas must not overlap.

Note There are several methods of improving the
electrode resistance to a lower value, either driving it
deeper into the soil (using extendable type rods) or
using chemicals such as common salt and sodium
carbonate.

89   Show diagrammatically how a polarity test is
     made on an Edison-type screw lampholder.

                                        Ex.12/Q5/Vol.1

Solution

See Figure 41.

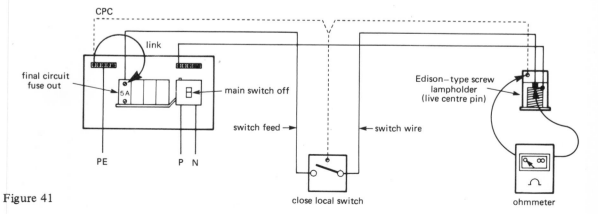

Figure 41

90 Show diagrammatically how one tests for insulation resistance on a portable electric drill. State ohmic values applicable to the test.

Ex.12/Q6/Vol.1

Solution

See Figure 42. Reference should be made to Regulation 613—8 of the IEE Wiring Regulations. Minimum value 0.5 MΩ.

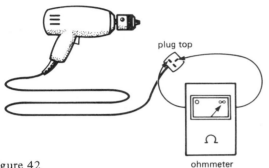

plug top

ohmmeter

Figure 42

91 A large installation was tested for insulation resistance and found to be 0.3 megohms. Explain the procedure you would take in trying to improve this reading or give reasons why the value is relatively low.

Ex.12/Q7/Vol.1

Solution

The ohmic value given in the question is insufficient to meet the requirements of Regulations 613—6 and 613—7 respectively, where for a completed installation the insulation resistance must not be less than 1 megohm.

As stated in Regulation 613—5, large installations may be divided into groups of outlets each containing not less than 50 outlets. It is quite possible in this instance that there are too many outlets being tested at once having the effect of lowering the test value since circuits are connected in parallel.

The remedy is to sectionalize the wiring and test on the basis described. There may be a possibility of one or more final circuits giving a higher than normal reading particularly when tested between *live* conductors.

92 Explain how you would identify the cores of a MIMS multicore cable and test it for insulation resistance.

Ex.12/Q8/Vol.1

Solution

In practice, the procedure is to use the metal sheath as a return conductor and connect one end of a tester (bell set or ohmmeter) to the sheath and the other end of the tester to individual cores. At the other end of the MIMS cable, cores are separately touched to the sheath and identified accordingly. Individual cores are then marked with tape or proper label to signify their circuit function.

If the tester chosen was an ohmmeter, then the insulation resistance to earth of each core could be ascertained. Care should be taken

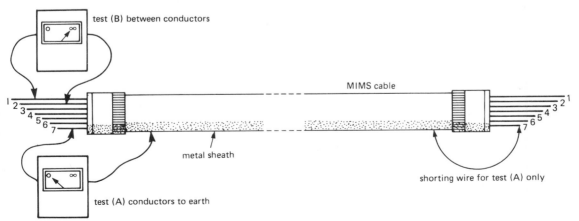

test (B) between conductors

MIMS cable

metal sheath

shorting wire for test (A) only

test (A) conductors to earth

Figure 43

when using the tester in view of it generating
500 V. In making the test, one should test
between cores in case any are touching each
other inside the termination glands. Figure 43
shows both methods. It will be noticed that
the continuity test is indicating towards zero
on the tester and the insulation test indicating
towards infinity meaning that there is an
exceedingly high value of resistance between
the cores.

93   A large electrical installation was subdivided
into five insulation resistance tests, namely:
0.8 megohm, 100 megohm, 20 megohm,
70 megohm and 2 megohm. What is the equivalent test result of the whole installation?
What is an 'outlet' as defined in Regulation
613–5?   Ex.12/Q9/Vol.1

Solution

This question qualifies the answer given in
Question 91 with regard to sectionalizing the
installation for separate insulation resistance
tests. The overall value is found by adding the
five test results, remembering that one is
dealing with parallel circuits. Hence:

$$\frac{1}{R} = \frac{1}{0.8} + \frac{1}{100} + \frac{1}{20} + \frac{1}{70} + \frac{1}{2}$$

$$= 1.25 + 0.01 + 0.05 + 0.014\,2 + 0.5$$

$$= 1.824$$

$$= \frac{1.824}{1}$$

Therefore:

$$\frac{R}{1} = \frac{1}{1.824} = \textbf{0.548 M}\Omega$$

It should be noted that this value is below 1
megohm as required for a completed installation. The first test reading should have indicated
this.
    The term 'outlet' refers to points of con-
nection where cables are broken, such as lighting
points, socket outlets, switch boxes etc.

94   When should the following installations be
inspected?

(a)   farms
(b)   petrol filling stations
(c)   construction sites
(d)   dwellings
(e)   caravan sites   Ex.12/Q10/Vol.1

Solution

Reference should be made to 'Inspection Certificate', page 191, Appendix 16 of the IEE
Wiring Regulations.

(a)   It is recommended that farms are inspected
       every three years.
(b)   It is often recommended that petrol
       stations are inspected every year.
(c)   For construction sites where temporary
       supplies are made available, the recom-
       mended period between inspections is
       three months.
(d)   It is recommended that dwellings are
       inspected every five years or less.
(e)   The recommended frequency for inspec-
       tion of caravan sites is every year, but
       certainly not less than every three years.

95   Describe with the aid of a diagram the operation
of a fluorescent lamp with its associated control-
gear.

Solution

The circuit is shown in Figure 44 and its operation is explained on page 67 of *Electrical
Installation Technology 1* and page 86 of
Electrical Installation Technology 2.
    It will be seen from the diagram that the
fluorescent tube circuit consists of a choke or
lamp ballast, power factor correction capacitor
and starter switch. The lamp ballast is in series
with the fluorescent tube while the starter
switch is connected across the tube electrodes
and the correction capacitor across the supply
terminals of the lamp circuit.
    When the circuit is connected to the supply,
a p.d. occurs across the starter switch contacts
which are bimetallic strip electrodes enclosed in
a neon filled glass tube. The p.d. causes the
neon to glow and heat up the electrodes so that
they come together and allow the passage of
current around the circuit. The current heats

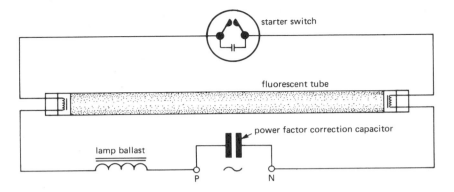

Figure 44

up both lamp electrodes but because no p.d. exists in the starter switch at this moment, its bimetallic contacts cool down and spring apart. The breaking of these contacts causes the choke to produce a momentary high voltage that is sufficient to strike an arc in the fluorescent tube and its internal phosphor coating converts ultra-violet radiation into visible light.

The starter switch is provided with a radio interference suppressor because of its contacts opening and closing, and the power factor correction capacitor is fitted because of the choke's poor power factor, making the circuit take more current than necessary.

96   Draw a simple diagram of a closed-circuit intruder alarm circuit consisting of four contact points, transformer, relay, indicator lamp and external bell.

Solution

See Figure 45.

97   Distinguish between:
(a)   *emergency lighting* and *escape lighting*
(b)   *maintained emergency lighting* and *non-maintained emergency lighting*.

Solution

(a)   Emergency lighting is a general term to denote lighting intended to allow occupants of a building to see in the event of normal lighting failure. Escape lighting by its implication, is emergency lighting, it ensures that the means of escape can be safely and effectively used at all material times.

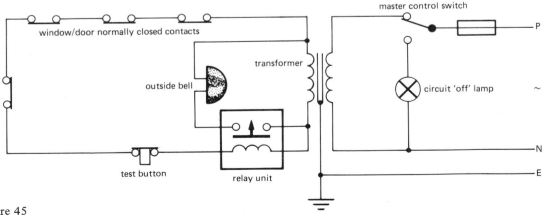

Figure 45

(b) A maintained emergency lighting system is one in which all emergency lamps are in operation at all material times, whereas a non-maintained emergency lighting system is one in which all emergency lamps are in operation only when the normal lighting fails.

98 Determine the assessed current demand of three 12 kW/240 V cooking appliances used in a boarding house.

Solution

Reference should be made to Table 4B, Appendix 4, IEE Wiring Regulations. Here it will be seen that there is no diversity allowed on the first cooking appliance, an 80% allowance on the second and 60% allowance on remaining appliances. Thus:

First appliance

$$I = \frac{P}{V} = \frac{12\ 000}{240} = 50 \text{ A}$$

Second appliance

$$I = \frac{P}{V} = \frac{12\ 000 \times 0.8}{240} = 40 \text{ A}$$

Third appliance

$$I = \frac{P}{V} = \frac{12\ 000 \times 0.6}{240} = 30 \text{ A}$$

The assessed current demand is therefore 50 + 40 + 30 = **120 A**

99 With the aid of a diagram explain the operation of an oven hotplate simmerstat.

Solution

The simmerstat controller is basically a variable heat switch or energy regulator and is shown in Figure 46. It will be seen that the supply phase connection is connected to a fixed contact while a moving contact conveys current through the heating element and also through a compensating bimetal and heater winding. A control cam adjusts the initial temperature required and its contact with the bimetallic strip only allows the lower leaf of the strip to

move away from the fixed contact. This occurs when the heater winding bends the bimetallic strip apart.

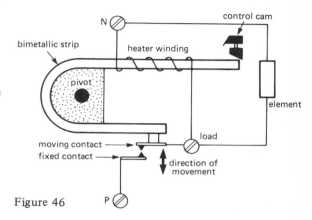

Figure 46

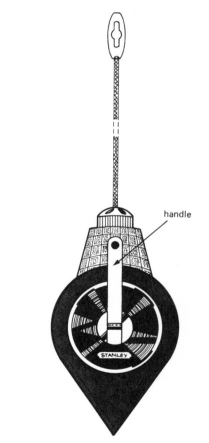

Figure 47 *Combined chalk line/plumb line kit*

100 Briefly provide notes on the subject of 'marking off' for vertical and horizontal alignment in preparation for fixing electrical apparatus and equipment.

Solution

There are several methods one can use for obtaining true vertical and horizontal alignment of electrical apparatus and associated equipment. Commonly used for vertical alignment is the *plumb line* or plum-bob and line which simply is a weight attached to a length of string or twine. The weight must be allowed to stop moving sideways when the string is held in position. The wall or structure is then marked at extreme ends on the string line. The practice then is to stretch a *chalk line* between the marks, plucking at the line in order to leave an identifiable vertical chalk mark so that fixings and supports can be fastened. Figure 47 is a typical chalk line kit which serves to keep the line continually loaded with chalk whenever the string is wound back into the spool.

Another useful tool is the *spirit level* used for both horizontal and vertical alignment, although the latter use might entail a plumb level. These tools consist of level glass tubes set in a straightedge. The tubes contain air bubbles and when located centrally between markings give the required alignments. Spirit levels are commonly used on apparatus and equipment before being fixed in position.

One last useful arrangement is a *water level*. This comprises two glass tubes connected together by a flexible rubber tube. The tube is filled with water until the level is halfway up both tubes. In this way it is possible to measure horizontal alignment on walls divided by partitions or even the opposite sides of a wall.

Part II
Certificate

Electrical science

Note Questions 101–23 are extracted from *Electrical Installation Technology 2*. Questions 124–50 are additional, based on the course syllabus.

---

101 Draw a diagram showing how a single-phase wattmeter, voltmeter and ammeter are connected to a resistive load. Assume the use of a current transformer in view of the load current being 300 A. Ex.3/Q9/Vol.2

Solution

See Figure 48.

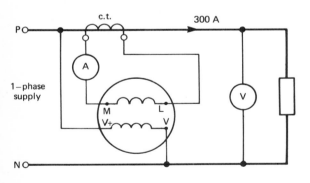

Figure 48

102 A 6.8 kW/415 V/50 Hz, three-phase induction motor has an efficiency of 85% and a power factor of 0.7 lagging. Determine the value of power factor correction capacitors to improve the power factor to unity condition.
Ex.3/Q10/Vol.2

Solution

Since efficiency (p.u.) = $\dfrac{\text{output}}{\text{input}}$

$$\text{input} = \frac{\text{output}}{\text{efficiency (p.u.)}}$$

$$= \frac{6.8}{0.85} = 8 \text{ kW}$$

Since kilovoltamperes = $\dfrac{\text{kW}}{\text{p.f.}}$

$$= \frac{8}{0.7} = 11.43 \text{ kVA}$$

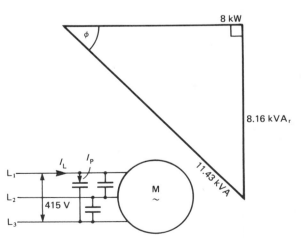

Figure 49

The lagging reactive $kVA_r = \sqrt{kVA^2 - kW^2}$

$$= \sqrt{11.43^2 - 8^2}$$

$$= 8.16 \text{ kVA}$$

For unity power factor conditions, the injected leading capacitive kVA_r must equal the lagging reactive kVA_r of 8.16 kVA. Thus:

$$I_L = \frac{kVA_r}{\sqrt{3}V_L}$$

$$= \frac{8160}{\sqrt{3}.415}$$

$$= 11.35 \text{ A}$$

Since $I_P = \dfrac{I_L}{\sqrt{3}}$

$$= \frac{11.35}{\sqrt{3}}$$

$$= 6.55 \text{ A}$$

Then X_C/phase $= \dfrac{V_L}{I_P}$

$$= \frac{415}{6.55}$$

$$= 63.35 \ \Omega$$

Thus C/phase $= \dfrac{10^6}{314.2 \times 63.35}$

$$= \textbf{50 } \boldsymbol{\mu}\textbf{F}$$

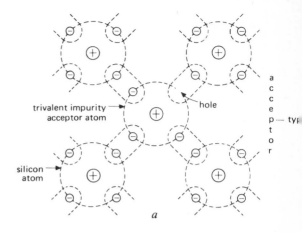

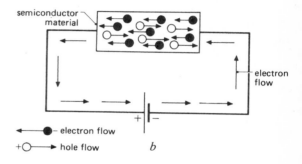

Figure 50   (a) *p-type material*
(b) *Fixed holes belonging to positive ions (arrows on holes indicate attraction to negative polarity of battery). Only electrons flow around circuit*

103 Draw a circuit diagram showing how conduction of holes occur in a piece of semiconductor p-type material connected to a battery.

Ex.4/Q1/Vol.2

Solution

See Figure 50.

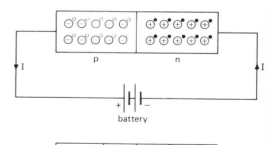

104 Explain what happens when forward and reverse bias is applied to a pn junction diode.

Ex.4/Q2/Vol.2

Solution

Reference should be made to the 'Diode', page 48 in *Electrical Installation Technology 2*. Figure 51 shows two conditions created by the battery connections. The *forward bias* connection is when the positive battery terminal is connected to the 'p' material while the negative

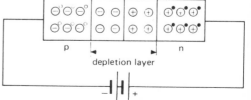

Figure 51

battery terminal is connected to the 'n' material. If the battery voltage is high enough it will destroy the internal barrier potential and allow electrons to pass into the 'p' material and flow around the circuit (electron flow). The pn junction diode is now in its 'on' state.

If the polarity of the battery connections to the diode is reversed as shown, then the electrons in the 'n' material are attracted towards the positive battery connection and holes in the 'p' material attracted towards the negative battery connection. This creates a wide depletion layer and very little current flows around the circuit. The diode is said to have *reverse bias* and is now in its 'off' state.

105 Draw the circuit diagram of a full-wave bridge rectifier unit which is used to charge a 12 V battery from a 240 V single-phase supply. Incorporate the necessary protection and ammeter to measure the rectified current.

Ex.4/Q3/Vol.2

Solution

See Figure 13, page 24.

106 Draw a circuit diagram of a simple d.c. motor circuit showing how thyristors can be used to control its operation. Ex.4/Q4/Vol.2

Solution

See Figure 52.

Note A full explanation of its operation is not required at this stage.

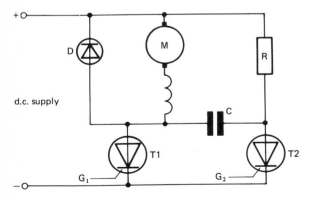

Figure 52

107 Explain the effects of leakage current in a semiconductor device. Ex.4/Q5/Vol.2

Solution

In a pn junction diode, when it is reverse biased, the current due to minority carriers (electrons produced by thermal agitation) soon reaches maximum value. This occurs when the minority carrier rate of flow equals the rate at which they are produced by thermal breakdown. Leakage current or saturation current is an undesirable flow of current across a reverse biased pn junction.

108 What is meant by the following in connection with a thyristor:
(a) peak forward voltage
(b) peak reverse voltage
(c) average forward current Ex.4/Q6/Vol.2

Solution

(a) Peak forward voltage is the voltage a thyristor will withstand without breakdown. Normally a thyristor is chosen to have a value twice that of the peak forward voltage.
(b) This is the maximum reverse voltage a thyristor can withstand without damage.
(c) This is the maximum forward current (I_F) a thyristor can pass.

109 What is a heat sink? Ex.4/Q7/Vol.2

Solution

Solid state devices, such as diodes and thyristors, while being robust in design may become damaged by excessive heat and temperature rise beyond their working performance. Because of this they are fitted with heat sinks as part of their assembly. These are usually a mass of metal, much larger than the device need be, with the purpose of dissipating any heat away from the device. Heat sinks may take various shapes and sizes, and devices fitted with cooling fins to increase the area of their radiating surface are quite common. See Figure 53.

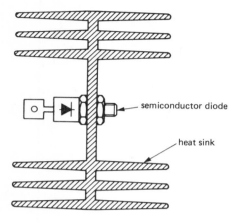

Figure 53

110 Give at least *four* applications for each of the following semiconductor devices:

    (a)   diode

    (b)   transistor

    (c)   thyristor

    (d)   triac

                         Ex.4/Q8/Vol.2

Solution

    (a)   battery charger rectifier;
            end of line diode in fire alarm system;
            motor control circuits, and
            electronic switching circuits.

    (b)   radio circuits;
            amplifier circuits;
            power control circuits, and
            opto-electronic devices.

    (c)   motor control circuits;
            instrumentation;
            electric fence control circuits, and
            electronic circuits.

    (d)   lighting dimmer circuits;
            proximity switches;
            heater control circuits, and
            electronic firing circuits.

111 Explain how full-wave rectification is obtained from a single-phase a.c. supply. Draw the a.c. voltage waveform and d.c. output voltage waveform.   Ex.4/Q9/Vol.2

Solution

There are commonly two methods of achieving full-wave rectification using pn junction diodes, (a) using a centre-tapped transformer and (b) using a bridge rectifier. The latter method has been shown, but Figure 54 shows the use

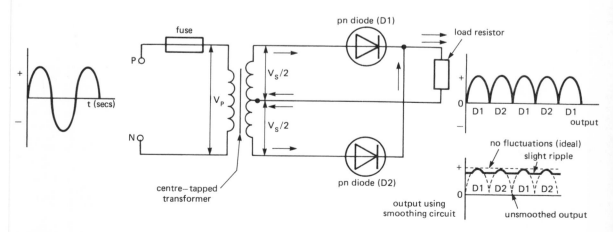

Figure 54

of two diodes connected to a centre-tapped transformer.

When diode D1 is positive, it will conduct in the forward direction through the load and back via the centre point of the transformer. The signal down to diode D2 is blocked. In the second half cycle, D2 conducts while D1 blocks and the output signal takes on the pattern shown. An improvement to the output signal is by using a smoothing circuit which raises the level of signal, making it steady with very little ripple.

112 What is meant by the following terms?
(a) depletion layer
(b) covalent bond
(c) current carrier
(d) breakdown voltage   Ex.4/Q10/Vol.2

Solution

These are all terms used in semiconductor devices and their meanings can be found on page 57 of *Electrical Installation Technology 2* along with other terms.

(a) This is the region in a semiconductor where there are no carriers (see current carriers below) but there exists a barrier potential of a few tenths of a volt.
(b) This is a bond formed by the interchange of valence electrons between atoms, i.e. electrons in the outer shells of atoms.
(c) Current carriers are mobile electrons and holes constituting an electric current. A hole being a mobile valency among valence electrons *only within* the semi-conductor material.
(d) The reverse voltage at which current begins to increase is called the breakdown voltage.

113 Using Figure 55(a), complete the resultant m.m.f. rotating magnetic field direction.
Ex.5/Q1/Vol.2

Solution

See Figure 55(b).

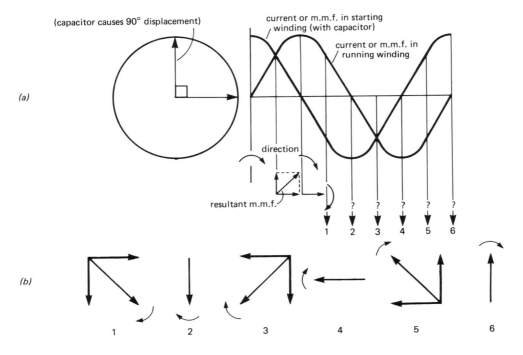

Figure 55

114 Determine the synchronous speed (n_s) and rotor speed (n_r) from the following induction motor data:

(a) $f = 50, p = 2$ and $s = 0.03$
(b) $f = 50, p = 4$ and $s = 0.03$
(c) $f = 50, p = 6$ and $s = 0.03$
(d) $f = 50, p = 6$ and $s = 0.05$
(e) $f = 60, p = 6$ and $s = 0.05$

Note f is the frequency of supply in hertz
p is the number of stator poles
s is the slip in per unit values

Ex.5/Q2/Vol.2

Solution

(a) $n_s = \dfrac{f}{p}$ $n_r = n_s(1 - s)$

$= \dfrac{50}{1}$ $= 50(1 - 0.03)$

$= \textbf{50 rev/s}$ $= \textbf{48.5 rev/s}$

(b) $n_s = \dfrac{50}{2}$ $n_r = 25(1 - 0.03)$

$= \textbf{25 rev/s}$ $= \textbf{24.25 rev/s}$

(c) $n_s = \dfrac{50}{3}$ $n_r = 16.66(1 - 0.03)$

$= \textbf{16.66 rev/s}$ $= \textbf{16.17 rev/s}$

(d) $n_s = \dfrac{50}{3}$ $n_r = 16.66(1 - 0.05)$

$= \textbf{16.66 rev/s}$ $= \textbf{15.83 rev/s}$

(e) $n_s = \dfrac{60}{3}$ $n_r = 20(1 - 0.05)$

$= \textbf{20 rev/s}$ $= \textbf{19 rev/s}$

115 (a) What is an interpole? Explain where it is connected in a machine.
(b) Draw a diagram of a d.c. machine's main salient pole showing both series and shunt field connections to give cumulative compound characteristics. Show current directions in the field windings and pole polarity.   Ex.5/Q3/Vol.2

Solution

(a) An interpole is a small pole fitted between the main poles of a d.c. machine

in order to neutralize the effects of armature reaction which causes sparking at the brushes. Interpoles are connected in series with the armature connections.

(b) See Figure 56, which is a main pole, not an interpole.

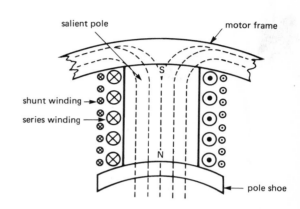

Figure 56

116 The speed of a 220 V d.c. motor with an armature current of 10 A and armature resistance 0.5 Ω is 12.5 rev/s. What would be its speed if the armature current was increased to 30 A? Assume the armature voltage (applied voltage) and field current remain unchanged.   Ex.5/Q4/Vol.2

Solution

Since $E = V - I_a R_a$

where E is the back e.m.f.
V is the applied volts
I_a is the armature current
R_a is the armature resistance

First condition:

$E_1 = 220 - (10 \times 0.5) = 215$ V

Second condition:

$E_2 = 220 - (30 \times 0.5) = 205$ V

The back e.m.f. is proportional to the speed of the armature and magnetic flux per pole. If the field current remains unchanged, the conditions can be represented by the expression:

$$E \propto \phi n$$

(See page 72 of *Electrical Installation Technology 2.*)

Thus $E_1 \propto n_1$

$$E_2 \propto n_2$$

By proportion $n_2 = \dfrac{n_1 \times E_2}{E_1}$

$$= \dfrac{12.5 \times 205}{215}$$

$$= \mathbf{11.9 \ rev/s}$$

117 Determine the efficiency and power factor of a single-phase motor having the following data:

Electrical input   — wattmeter reading 13 120 W
voltmeter reading 240 V
ammeter reading 74 A

Mechanical output — 11 190 W

Ex.5/Q5/Vol.2

Solution

$$\text{efficiency} = \dfrac{\text{output}}{\text{input}}$$

$$= \dfrac{11\ 190}{13\ 120}$$

$$= \mathbf{0.85 \ p.u. \ (85\%)}$$

$$\text{power factor} = \dfrac{\text{input power}}{\text{voltamperes}}$$

$$= \dfrac{13\ 120}{240 \times 74}$$

$$= \mathbf{0.74 \ lagging}$$

118 Determine the power output, power factor and efficiency of a three-phase motor having the following test data:

1   speed 23.75 rev/s
2   input wattmeter reading 16 920 W
3   voltmeter reading 400 V
4   ammeter reading 39.5 A
5   brake pulley diameter 0.33 m
6   effective pull at circumference of pulley 564.44N   Ex.5/Q9/Vol.2

Solution

Power output (mechanical) is given by the expression:

$$P_o = 2\pi.nT \text{ watts}$$

$$= 2 \times 3.142 \times 23.75 \times (564.44 \times 0.165)$$

$$= 13\ 899 \text{ W or } \mathbf{13.9 \ kW}$$

Note $T = F \times$ radius

$$\text{efficiency} = \dfrac{\text{output}}{\text{input}}$$

$$= \dfrac{13\ 899}{16\ 920}$$

$$= \mathbf{0.82 \ p.u. \ (82\%)}$$

and input (electrical) is given by the expression:

$$P_i = \sqrt{3} V_L I_L \cos \phi \text{ watts}$$

where $\cos \phi$ is the power factor

By transposition:

$$\cos \phi = \dfrac{P_i}{\sqrt{3} V_L I_L}$$

$$= \dfrac{16\ 920}{1.732 \times 400 \times 39.5}$$

$$= \mathbf{0.62 \ lagging}$$

119 The current taken by a 240 V, 50 Hz single-phase induction motor is 39 A at a power factor lagging of 0.75. Determine:

(a)   the input power in kilowatts
(b)   the kilovoltamperes
(c)   the size of capacitor which will raise the power factor to unity

Ex.5/Q10/Vol.2

Solution

(a) $P = VI\cos \phi$

$$= 240 \times 39 \times 0.75$$

$$= 7\ 020 \text{ W}$$

$$= \mathbf{7.02 \ kW}$$

(b) $VI = 240 \times 39$

$$= 9\ 360 \text{ VA}$$

$$= \mathbf{9.36 \ kVA}$$

(c) $C = \dfrac{10^6}{2\pi f X_c}\ \mu F$ but $X_c = \dfrac{V}{I_c}$

where X_c is the capacitive reactance
V is the supply voltage
I_c is the capacitive current

Since V is known, I_c must be found. The usual way to do this is by the formula:

$$I_c = \frac{VI_r}{V}$$

Here the VI_r represents the reactive voltamperes (or leading VA injected by the capacitors) to bring power factor to unity. For simplicity see Figure 57.

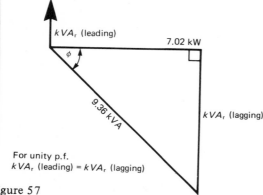

For unity p.f.
kVA_r (leading) = kVA_r (lagging)

Figure 57

Hence $kVA_r = \sqrt{kVA^2 - kW^2}$

$= \sqrt{9.36^2 - 7.02^2}$

$= \sqrt{38.33}$

$= 6.19\ kVA$

therefore $I_c = \dfrac{VI_r}{V}$

$= \dfrac{6\ 190}{240}$

$= 25.79\ A$

and $X_c = \dfrac{V}{I_c}$

$= \dfrac{240}{25.79}$

$= 9.3\ \Omega$

thus $C = \dfrac{10^6}{2 \times 50 \times 9.3}$

$= 342\ \mu F$

---

120 Determine the illuminance on the surface directly below an incandescent lamp of 1 200 cd if the distance is:
(a)   3 m
(b)   6 m
(c)   9 m   Ex.6/Q7/Vol.2

Solution

(a) $E = \dfrac{I}{d^2}$ lux

$= \dfrac{1\ 200}{9}$

$= 133.3\ lx$

(b) $E = \dfrac{1\ 200}{36}$

$= 33\ lx$

(c) $E = \dfrac{1\ 200}{81}$

$= 14.8\ lx$

121 With reference to Figure 58, determine the illuminance at point C.   Ex.6/Q8/Vol.2

Solution

See Figure 58.

$$E = \frac{I}{h^2}\cos\phi$$

where h is the distance 6 m

$$E = \frac{900}{36} \times 0.707$$

$= 17.67\ lx$

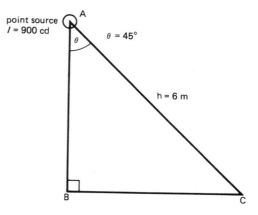

Figure 58

122 Calculate the average illuminance in a room measuring 10.5 m by 7 m, assuming the light output of each luminaire lighting the room to be 5 000 lm with utilization factor and maintenance factor 0.5 and 0.8 respectively. Sixteen luminaires are installed.

Ex.6/Q9/Vol.2

Solution

The average illuminance required is given by the expression:

$$E = \frac{F \times MF \times CU}{A}$$

where F is the lumen output of luminaires
MF is the maintenance factor
CU is the coefficient of utilization
A is the area required to be lit

$$E = \frac{(5\ 000 \times 16) \times 0.8 \times 0.5}{10.5 \times 7}$$

$$= \textbf{435.4 lx}$$

123 Two incandescent filament lamps of luminous intensity 100 cd and 60 cd respectively in all directions are fixed to the ends of a photometer bench as shown in Figure 59. A movable, double-sided, white matt screen is placed between the lamps with its opposite faces normal to the rays from the lamps. The face opposite the 60 cd lamp receives an illuminance of 26 lx and the other side receives an illuminance of 67 lx. Find:
(a) the distance each lamp is from the screen
(b) the illuminance on each side of the screen when it is placed halfway between the lamps   Ex.6/Q10/Vol.2

Solution

(a) Since $E = \dfrac{I}{d^2}$

By transposition: $d^2 = \dfrac{I}{E}$

Thus:

$$d_1 = \sqrt{\frac{I_1}{E_1}} = \sqrt{\frac{100}{67}} = 1.22 \text{ m}$$

and:

$$d_2 = \sqrt{\frac{I_2}{E_2}} = \sqrt{\frac{60}{26}} = 1.52 \text{ m}$$

(b) Since $d = d_1 + d_2$

$$= 1.22 + 1.52$$
$$= 2.74 \text{ m}$$

The screen positioned halfway would be

$$\frac{2.74}{2} = 1.37 \text{ m}$$

Thus:

$$E_1 = \frac{I_1}{d^2} = \frac{100}{1.876\ 9} = 53 \text{ lx}$$

and:

$$E_2 = \frac{I_2}{d^2} = \frac{60}{1.876\ 9} = 32 \text{ lx}$$

124 With reference to Figure 59, assuming the distance between the lamps to be 2.74 m, what position has the screen to be moved to in order to provide equal illumination on both sides?

Solution

In this case $E_1 = E_2$

i.e. $\dfrac{I_1}{d_1^2} = \dfrac{I_2}{d_2^2}$

By transposition: $\dfrac{I_1}{I_2} = \left(\dfrac{d_1}{d_2}\right)^2$

Thus: $\sqrt{\dfrac{100}{60}} = \dfrac{d_1}{d_2}$

$$1.29 = \frac{d_1}{d_2}$$

$$1.29 d_2 = d_1$$

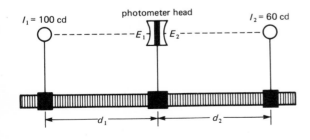

I_1 = 100 cd   photometer head I_2 = 60 cd

Figure 59

Since
$$d = d_1 + d_2$$
$$= 2.74 \text{ m}$$
$$d_1 = 2.74 - d_2$$

There are now two conditions for d_1

$$1.29d_2 = 2.74 - d_2$$
$$d_2 + 1.29d_2 = 2.74$$
$$2.29d_2 = 2.74$$
$$d_2 = \frac{2.74}{2.29}$$
$$= 1.196 \text{ m}$$

Therefore:

$$d_1 = 2.74 - 1.196$$
$$= 1.544 \text{ m}$$

125 (a) For the circuit shown in Figure 60 the value of R is 12 Ω and the value of X_L is 16 Ω. Calculate the:
   (i) impedance of the circuit
   (ii) current
   (iii) voltage across each component
(b) Draw a phasor diagram showing the phase relation between the current, the supply voltage and the voltages across the resistor and inductor.
(c) From the phasor diagram, or otherwise determine:
   (i) the phase angle between current and supply voltage
   (ii) the power factor

CGLI/II/1983

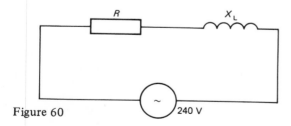

Figure 60

Solution

(i) $Z = \sqrt{R^2 + X_L^2}$
$$= \sqrt{12^2 + 16^2}$$
$$= 20 \ \Omega$$

(a) (ii) $I = \dfrac{V}{Z} = \dfrac{240}{20} = \textbf{12 A}$

(iii) $V_R = IR = 12 \times 12 = 144 \text{ V}$
$V_L = IX_L = 12 \times 16 = 192 \text{ V}$

Check:
$$V_S = \sqrt{V_R{}^2 + V_L{}^2}$$
$$= \sqrt{144^2 + 192^2}$$
$$= \textbf{240 V}$$

(b) See Figure 61.

(c) (i) Use protractor or use formula:
$$\cos \phi = \frac{R}{Z} \text{ and find phase angle } (\phi)$$
$$= \textbf{53}°$$

(ii) Power factor $= \dfrac{R}{Z} = \dfrac{12}{20} = \textbf{0.6 lagging}$

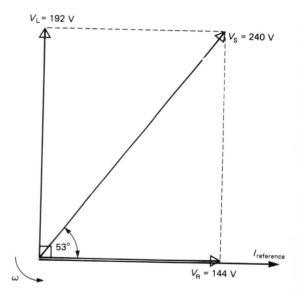

Figure 61

126 (a) Explain with the aid of diagrams the method of reversing the direction of rotation of *each* of the following types of motor:
   (i) three-phase induction
   (ii) single-phase capacitor start
   (iii) d.c. shunt
   (iv) series

(b) Calculate the full load current of a 48 kW 3-phase 415 V motor given that the efficiency and power factor at full load is 85% and 0.9 respectively

CGLI/II/83

Solution

(a) Methods of reversing the direction of rotation of motors are given on page 74 of *Electrical Installation Technology 2.*

   (i)   Change any two supply leads

   (ii)   Change connections of running winding *or* starting winding

   (iii)   Change connections of shunt field winding *or* armature winding

   (iv)   Change connections of series field winding *or* armature winding

   See Figure 62.

(b) $\text{efficiency} = \dfrac{\text{output}}{\text{input}}$

By transposition:

$$\text{input} = \frac{\text{output}}{\text{efficiency}}$$

$$= \frac{48\,000}{0.85}$$

$$= \mathbf{56.47\ kW}$$

Since input $(P) = \sqrt{3}\,V_L I_L \cos\phi$

By transposition:

$$I_L = \frac{P}{\sqrt{3}\,V_L \cos\phi}$$

$$= \frac{56\,470}{\sqrt{3} \times 415 \times 0.9}$$

$$= \mathbf{87.29\ A}$$

127   A 1 kW, 240 V, 50 Hz, 2 pole single-phase, induction motor operates with 5% slip, 75% efficiency and 0.7 power factor on full load.

  (a)   Draw a labelled circuit diagram of a push button starter with undervoltage and overcurrent protection for the above motor.

  (b)   For full load conditions calculate the:

    (i)   input power and current

    (ii)   motor speed   CGLI/II/83

Solution

(a)   See Figure 63.

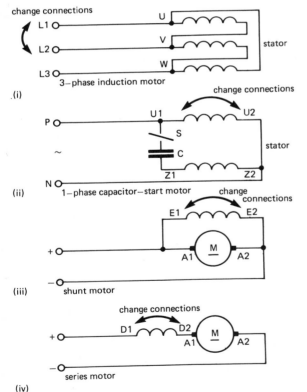

Figure 62

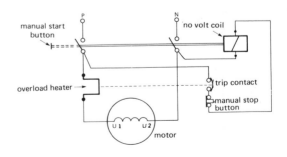

Figure 63

(b)   (i)   Since

$$\text{efficiency} = \frac{\text{output}}{\text{input}}$$

then

$$\text{input} = \frac{\text{output}}{\text{efficiency (p.u.)}}$$

$$= \frac{1\,000}{0.75}$$

$$= 1.33 \text{ kW}$$

because

$$\text{input} = V_P I_P \cos \phi$$

By transposition:

$$I = \frac{P}{V_P \cos \phi}$$

$$= \frac{1\,333.3}{240 \times 0.7}$$

$$= 7.94 \text{ A}$$

(ii)   Since $n_s = \dfrac{f}{p}$

$$= \frac{50}{1}$$

$$= 50 \text{ rev/s}$$

where n_s is the synchronous speed
      f is the supply frequency
      p is the number of pairs of poles

and $n_r = n_s(1 - s)$

where n_r is the rotor speed
      s is the per unit slip

Thus: $n_r = 50(1 - 0.05)$

$$= 47.5 \text{ rev/s}$$

128   A moving coil milli-ammeter has a resistance of 5 Ω with full scale deflection at 15 mA. The scale reads 0–15 mA with 15 divisions.
(a)   With the aid of circuit diagrams explain how:
     (i)   the current range of the instrument may be extended
     (ii)   the milli-ammeter can be adapted for use as a voltmeter
(b)   (i)   Calculate the value of the resistor required to enable the milli-ammeter to read 0–3 A.

(ii)   By what factor must the scale reading be multiplied to give correct readings of current?
(c)   (i)   Calculate the value of the resistor required to enable the milli-ammeter to read 0–150 V.
     (ii)   How many volts will one division of the scale now represent?

CGLI/II/80

Solution

(a)   See Figure 64.
     (i)   To extend the range of the milli-ammeter to read more current, a resistor called a *shunt* is used. This component is wired or fitted across the milli-ammeter's terminals (i.e. *shunted* across). The shunt resistor is very often of a low ohmic value since it allows a large proportion of the circuit current to pass. The instrument will not be damaged provided the correct value of shunt is determined. The scale reading will also need modifying.
     (ii)   To extend the range of the milli-ammeter to read voltage, a resistor called a *multiplier* is used.

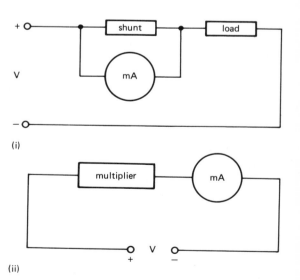

Figure 64

This component is wired or fitted in series with the instrument. The multiplier resistor is very often of a high ohmic value in order to limit the current flowing through the instrument up to full scale deflection. The scale will have to be changed so that it reads voltage.

(b) The calculations are as follows:

(i) If the instrument has to be modified to read 3 A, then the shunt resistor must take the difference between this reading and the f.s.d. value of 15 mA, i.e. $3 - 0.015 = 2.985$ A.

Since the potential difference will be the same across the shunt as it is across the instrument for f.s.d. then finding the p.d. will help find the value of the shunt. Thus:

$$\text{p.d.} = I_{\text{f.s.d.}} \times R_{\text{inst.}}$$
$$= 0.015 \times 5$$
$$= 75 \text{ mV}$$

$$\text{Shunt} = \frac{\text{p.d.}}{\text{shunt current}}$$
$$= \frac{0.075}{2.985}$$
$$= 0.025 \ \Omega$$

(ii) The factor required is found by simply dividing the instrument's f.s.d. reading into 3 A, i.e.

$$\frac{3}{0.015} = 200.$$

(c) (i) The value of multiplier resistor is found by firstly finding the p.d. across it, then dividing by the instrument's f.s.d. of 15 mA. Thus:

$$\text{p.d.} = 150 - 0.075$$
$$= 149.925 \text{ V}$$

$$\text{Multiplier} = \frac{\text{p.d.}}{I_{\text{f.s.d.}}}$$
$$= \frac{149.925}{0.015}$$
$$= 9\ 995 \ \Omega$$

(ii) Each scale division of the instrument will represent

$$\frac{150 \text{ V}}{15} = 10 \text{ volts}$$

129 A workshop is supplied from a 415/240 V three-phase 4-wire a.c. system.

(a) Explain the advantages of using a three-phase 4-wire system instead of a single-phase system for this type of premises.

(b) It is desired to measure the power factor of a single-phase motor installed in the workshop using an ammeter, voltmeter and wattmeter.

    (i) Draw a diagram showing the connections for all the instruments.

    (ii) Calculate the power factor of the motor if the readings on the instruments are 6 amperes, 240 volts and 1 008 watts respectively.

CGLI/II/80

Solution

(a) There are a number of advantages using a three-phase system over a single-phase system, they are:

    (i) A higher voltage is obtained which allows greater flexibility with installed plant, e.g. 3-phase motors can be used instead of 1-phase motors, two-phase welding equipment can be used and larger capacity plant can be used.

    (ii) Three-phase motors and other plant as well as lighting can be spread over three-phases to balance the system.

    (iii) Any out-of-balance load currents occurring in the system will flow down the neutral and keep the system balanced.

    (iv) Volt drop problems are reduced.

    (v) Stroboscopic effects can be eliminated using three-phase supplies when the lighting is discharge lighting.

(b) (i) See Figure 65.

(ii) power factor = $\dfrac{\text{power}}{\text{voltamperes}}$

$= \dfrac{1\ 008}{240 \times 6}$

= **0.7 lagging**

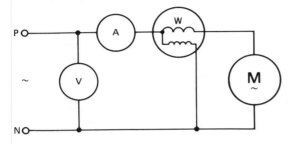

Figure 65

130 (a) Explain briefly how the back e.m.f. and the current change during the starting of a d.c. motor.

(b) A 200 V shunt-wound motor has an armature resistance of 0.25 Ω and a field resistance of 200 Ω. The motor gives an output of 4 kW at an efficiency of 80%. For this load calculate:
  (i) the motor power input in kW
  (ii) the load current
  (iii) the motor field current
  (iv) the armature current
  (v) the back e.m.f.

(c) What are the IEE requirements for the rating of fuses protecting a circuit feeding a motor?

CGLI/II/81

Solution

(a) The back e.m.f. of a d.c. motor is a generated e.m.f. created by the armature conductors cutting the main field as the armature revolves. This induced e.m.f. acts in opposition to the supply voltage and is always less than the supply voltage – the difference being the armature voltage drop.

As the armature accelerates, its back e.m.f. increases and the armature decreases. Also, as the load current increases, the back e.m.f. decreases. If the armature stops revolving there will be no back e.m.f. and with the supply switched on, excessive current will be drawn by the motor.

(b) (i) Since efficiency = $\dfrac{\text{output}}{\text{input}}$

input = $\dfrac{\text{output}}{\text{efficiency (p.u.)}}$

$= \dfrac{4\ 000}{0.8}$

= 5 000 W

= **5 kW**

(ii) $I_L = \dfrac{\text{power input}}{\text{supply voltage}}$

$= \dfrac{5\ 000}{200}$

= **25 A**

(iii) $I_f = \dfrac{\text{supply voltage}}{\text{field resistance}}$

$= \dfrac{200}{200}$

= **1 A**

(iv) Since $I_L = I_a + I_f$

then $I_a = I_L - I_f$

$= 25 - 1$

= **24 A**

(v) $E_b = V - I_a R_a$

$= 200 - (24 \times 0.25)$

= **194 V**

(c) Reference should be made to the IEE Wiring Regulations (15th Edition), Section 434, Reg. 434–5. In the 14th Edition, Reg. A–68 allowed fuses to be rated up to twice that of the cables between the fuse and the starter provided the starter afforded overload protection. However, the new requirements allow the use of an overload device complying with Section 433 to protect the conductors on the load side of the device, provided that it has a rated breaking capacity not less than the prospective short circuit current at the point of installation.

Note While it is not required in the question, Figure 66 is a diagram of a shunt motor showing some of the terms mentioned in the solution above.

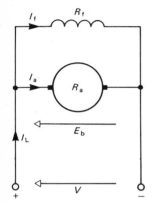

Important expressions

$$E_b \propto \phi n$$

$$E_b = V - I_a R_a$$

Legend

V is the supply voltage
I_L is the load current
I_a is the armature current
I_f is the shunt field current
R_a is the armature resistance
R_f is the shunt field resistance
E_b is the back e.m.f.

Figure 66

131 (a) Describe briefly the following parts of a d.c. motor:
  (i) armature
  (ii) commutator
  (iii) field system
 (b) Draw a circuit diagram for:
  (i) a d.c. series motor
  (ii) a d.c. compound motor

CGLI/II/82

Solution

(a) (i) The armature is the name for the rotating part of the machine and is made up of many laminations of soft-magnetic-alloy material into which armature coils are assembled.

  (ii) The commutator is part of the armature, serving the purpose of transferring an external current to the armature conductors via brush-gear.

(iii) The field system is that part of the d.c. motor which produces the excitation flux. It comprises the main poles and field windings which identify the machine as a *series*, *shunt* or *compound motor*.

(b) (i) See Figure 67(a).
  (ii) See Figure 67(b).

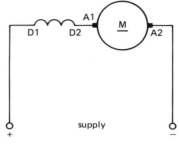

(a)

(b)

A1 – A2 armature connections
D1 – D2 series field connections
E1 – E2 shunt field connections

Figure 67

132 A factory supply is 11 kV, three-phase 3-wire and is fed to a transformer whose output is 415/240 V three-phase.
 (a) Draw a circuit diagram of this system.
 (b) What is the purpose of earthing the star point of the transformer?
 (c) Determine the total kVA load on the transformer if the following three-phase balanced loads were connected:
  (i) 120 kW heating load at unity power factor
  (ii) 240 kVA load at 0.8 power factor lagging

CGLI/II/80

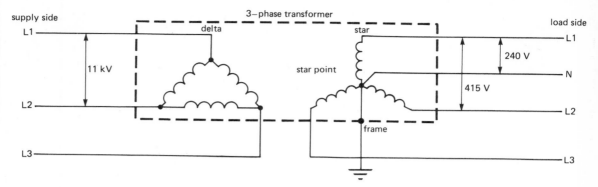

Figure 68

Solution

(a)   See Figure 68.

(b)   The purpose of earthing the star point of the transformer is to stabilize the distribution system in order to obtain a neutral connection to allow a lower and safer voltage, phase voltage, to be used for single-phase supplies. Also, any out-of-balance phase currents flowing in the system, as a result of mixed loads, will flow into the neutral conductor and by doing this will keep the system voltage balanced.

(c)   (i)   For unity power factor conditions, kW = kVA = 120 kW.

(ii)   For 0.8 power factor conditions, kW = 240 × 0.8 = 192 kW.

Adding these two conditions, the active power is 312 kW. The reactive kilovolt-amperes of (ii) is:

$$kVA_r = \sqrt{kVA^2 - kW^2}$$

$$= \sqrt{240^2 - 192^2}$$

$$= 144 \text{ kVA}$$

Thus total kVA $= \sqrt{312^2 + 144^2}$

$$= 343.6 \text{ kVA}$$

See Figure 69 for circuit phasor diagram.

133 (a)   State the conditions necessary to produce resonance in the circuit shown in Figure 70.

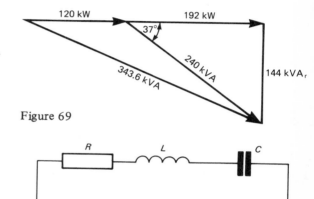

Figure 69

Figure 70

(b)   If the resistance of $R = 8\ \Omega$ and the inductive reactance of $L = 15\ \Omega$ determine the value of capacitance for resonance to occur.

Solution

(a)   For resonance to occur X_L must equal X_C.

(b)   Since $X_L = 15\ \Omega$, then $X_C = 15\ \Omega$

Thus $X_C = \dfrac{1}{2\pi f C}$

By transposition:

$$C = \frac{10^6}{2\pi F X_C}\ \mu F$$

$$= \frac{10^6}{314.2 \times 15}$$

$$= 212\ \mu F$$

134 If the capacitor in Figure 70 had a value of 100 μF and the supply voltage was 240 V determine:

(a) the circuit current if R and X_L were the same as before

(b) the power factor of the circuit

Solution

(a) First: $X_C = \dfrac{10^6}{2\pi f C}$

$= \dfrac{10^6}{314.2 \times 100}$

$= 31.8 \, \Omega$

second, since $Z = \sqrt{R^2 + (X_C - X_L)^2}$

$= \sqrt{64 + 282.24}$

$= 18.6 \, \Omega$

then: $I = \dfrac{V}{Z}$

$= \dfrac{240}{18.6}$

$= \mathbf{12.9 \, A}$

(b) Power factor $= \dfrac{R}{Z}$

$= \dfrac{8}{18.6}$

$= \mathbf{0.43 \, leading}$

135 Draw a phasor diagram of Figure 71 and find the value of supply current and power factor.

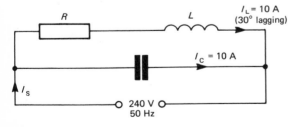

Figure 71

Solution

See Figure 72.

$I_S = \mathbf{10 \, A}$ leading the voltage by 30°

Power factor $(\cos \phi) = \cos 30^\circ = \mathbf{0.866 \, leading}$

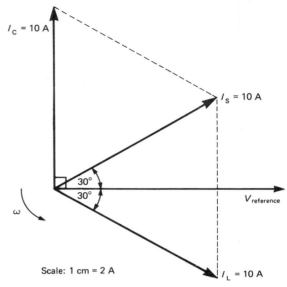

Scale: 1 cm = 2 A

Figure 72

136 Draw a phasor diagram of Figure 73 and determine the supply current and power factor.

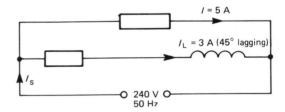

Figure 73

Solution

See Figure 74.

$I_S = \mathbf{7.4 \, A}$ (by measurement) lagging the voltage by 17°

Power factor $(\cos \phi) = \cos 17^\circ = \mathbf{0.956 \, lagging}$

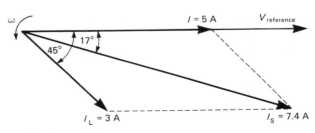

Scale: 1 cm = 1 A

Figure 74

137 From Figure 75, determine the value of the resistor marked X if the p.d. across the 2 Ω resistor is 60 V.

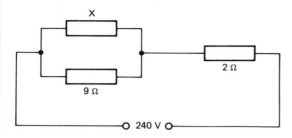

Figure 75

Solution

The current flowing through the circuit is found by:

$$I = \frac{V_2}{R} = \frac{60}{2} = 30 \text{ A}$$

Since $E = V_1 + V_2$

where E is the supply voltage
          V_1 and V_2 are the circuit p.d.s

then $V_1 = E - V_2$

$$= 240 - 60$$

$$= 180 \text{ V}$$

The current through the 9 Ω resistor is:

$$I = \frac{V_1}{R} = \frac{180}{9} = 20 \text{ A}$$

The current through the unknown resistor is:

$$30 - 20 = 10 \text{ A}$$

The value of the unknown resistor is:

$$R_X = \frac{V_1}{I} = \frac{180}{10} = \textbf{18 } \Omega$$

138 A 50 kW a.c. motor operates at a power factor of 0.65 lagging and an efficiency of 83%. A 40 kVA$_r$ power factor improvement capacitor is connected in parallel with the motor. Find graphically or by calculation the:
(a)   full load input kVA to the motor
(b)   supply kVA and power factor when the motor is run on
   (i)   full load
   (ii)   no load   CGLI/II/82

Solution

(a)   Motor's input $= \dfrac{\text{output}}{\text{efficiency (p.u.)}}$

$$= \frac{50}{0.83}$$

$$= 60.24 \text{ kW}$$

motor's VI $= \dfrac{P}{\text{p.f.}}$

$$= \frac{60.24}{0.65}$$

$$= 92.677 \text{ kVA}$$

The motor's lagging reactive component is:

$$kVA_r = \sqrt{kVA^2 - kW^2}$$

$$= \sqrt{92.677^2 - 60.24^2}$$

$$= 70.43 \text{ kVA}$$

Since 40 kVA$_r$ is injected, the remaining lagging kVA$_r$ is **30.43 kVA**

(b)   (i)   Full load kVA $= \sqrt{kW^2 + kVA_r{}^2}$

$$= \sqrt{60.24^2 + 30.43^2}$$

$$= \textbf{67.49 kVA}$$

(ii)   No load conditions assumes that no capacitors are connected and in this case the kilovoltamperes = **92.677 kVA**

Note   Figure 76 is a graphical solution. Also, if the motor is a cage induction motor, it will have a poor power factor on no-load.

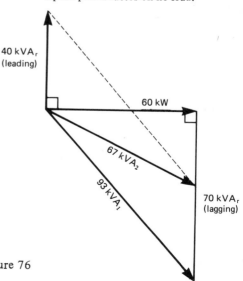

Figure 76

139 A 6-pole, 415 V, 50 Hz, three-phase induction motor operates at 0.7 power factor lagging and drives an elevator lifting 100 kg at a rate of 3.6 m/sec. If the elevator has an efficiency of 75% and the motor an efficiency of 85%, determine for full load conditions:

  (a) the motor's output and input

  (b) the motor's line current and phase current assuming the windings are delta connected

  (c) the motor's synchronous speed and rotor speed assuming a 0.05 p.u. slip

Solution

  (a) Work done/second = force × distance

$$= 100 \times 3.6$$

$$= 360 \text{ kgf}$$

If 1 kgf = 9.81 N, then power required by elevator is:

$$9.81 \times 360 = 3\,531.6 \text{ W}$$

motor's output = elevator's input (see Figure 77)

$$= \frac{3\,531.6 \times 100}{75}$$

$$= 4\,708.8 \text{ W}$$

motor's input $= \dfrac{4\,708.8 \times 100}{85}$

$$= 5\,539.76 \text{ W}$$

  (b) Since $\quad P = \sqrt{3}\,V_L I_L \cos \phi$

then $\quad I_L = \dfrac{P}{\sqrt{3}\,V_L \cos \phi}$

$$= \frac{5\,539.76}{\sqrt{3} \times 415 \times 0.7}$$

$$= 10.13 \text{ A}$$

$$I_P = \frac{I_L}{\sqrt{3}}$$

$$= \frac{10.13}{\sqrt{3}}$$

$$= 5.85 \text{ A}$$

  (c) $\qquad n_s = \dfrac{f}{p}$

$$= \frac{50}{3}$$

$$= 16.66 \text{ rev/s}$$

$$n_r = n_s(1 - s)$$

$$= 16.66(1 - 0.05)$$

$$= 15.83 \text{ rev/s}$$

140 Find the time required for an immersion heater to raise the temperature of 30 litres of water from 20 °C to 70 °C if the heating element is 3 kW, 240 V and the heating system is 82% efficient. Assume the heat specific capacity of water to be 4180 J/kg °C.

Solution

heat energy required $= mc(\theta_2 - \theta_1)$

$$= 30 \times 4\,180 \times 50$$

$$= 6.27 \times 10^6 \text{ J}$$

electrical energy required $= \dfrac{6.27 \times 10^6 \times 100}{82}$

$$= 7.646 \times 10^6 \text{ J}$$

time $= \dfrac{\text{electrical energy}}{\text{power}}$

$$= \frac{7.646 \times 10^6}{3\,000}$$

$$= 2\,548.8 \text{ s}$$

$$= 43 \text{ mins (approx.)}$$

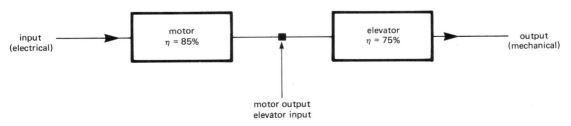

Figure 77

141   A machine is driven at 10 rev/s by a belt from a motor which is running at a speed of 25 rev/s. If the motor is fitted with a pulley of diameter 176 mm, find the size of pulley for the machine and belt speed assuming no slip.

Solution

The arrangement is shown in Figure 78. The expression used for the relationship between motor and machine pulley speeds and diameters is:

$$\frac{\text{speed of driven pulley } (n_1)}{\text{speed of driver pulley } (n_2)} = \frac{\text{diameter of driver pulley } (D_2)}{\text{diameter of driven pulley } (D_1)}$$

In this case:

$$n_1 = 10 \text{ rev/s}$$
$$n_2 = 25 \text{ rev/s}$$
$$D_1 =$$
$$D_2 = 176 \text{ mm}$$

Thus:

$$D_1 = \frac{D_2 \times n_2}{n_1}$$

$$= \frac{176 \times 25}{10}$$

$$= 440 \text{ mm}$$

speed of belt $= \pi \times$ diameter $\times$ speed of pulley

$$= \pi \times 176 \times 25 \text{ (using motor data)}$$

$$= 13\ 824.8 \text{ mm/s}$$

$$= \textbf{13.8 m/s}$$

D_2 = 176 mm
n_2 = 25 rev/s

D_1 = x mm
n_1 = 10 rev/s

belt

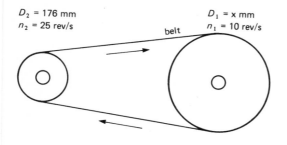

Figure 78

142   (a)   Draw a circuit diagram showing how a voltage transformer and current transformer are connected in a single-phase supply system so that a wattmeter can be used to measure power. Assume the system to be at a high voltage and taking a large load current.

     (b)   Briefly state some advantages of using a current and voltage instrument transformer.

Solution

(a)   See Figure 79.

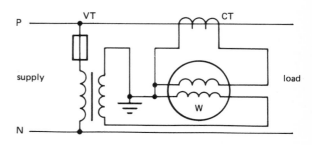

Figure 79

(b)   A current transformer is used where the circuit current is very high. Its secondary connection can be taken to a normal size instrument using much smaller cables, allowing the instrument to be read some distance from the actual measuring point.

     A voltage transformer is used to measure a proportion of the system's high voltage, again, using much smaller size cables. It is usual to find the secondary windings of current transformers catering for 5 A circuits and voltage transformer secondary windings catering for 110 V circuits.

143   Figure 80 shows the connections of a SON discharge lamp. With switch S open, ammeter A_1 reads 5 A and W reads 420 W. With S closed A_2 reads 2.2 A and A_1 reads 3 A, W reads 420 W again.

     (a)   Draw a phasor diagram of the circuit using 1 A = 2 cm.

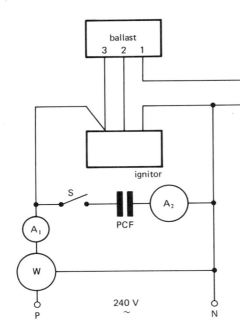

Figure 80

(b) If the lamp emits 44 000 lm and losses in the circuit are 20 W, what is the efficacy of the lamp?

Solution

(a) See Figure 81.

Note Since power factor $= \dfrac{P}{VI} = \dfrac{420}{240 \times 5} = 0.35$ lagging, the phase angle (θ) is $69°30'$ (approx.).

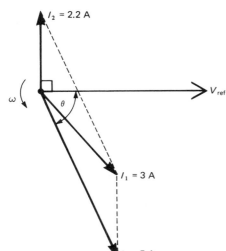

Figure 81

(b) The lamp is a 400 W SON and its efficacy is given by the expression:

$$\frac{\text{lumens}}{\text{watts}} = \frac{44\ 000}{400} = \mathbf{110\ lm/w}$$

144 With reference to Figure 82 showing the phasor relationship between red, yellow and blue phases of a 3-phase, 4-wire supply system, find by graphical construction the current flowing into the neutral if the current in the:

(a) red phase is 30 A and *in-phase* with V_R

(b) yellow phase is 20 A and *leading* $20°$ in front of V_Y

(c) blue phase is 25 A and *lagging* $10°$ behind V_B

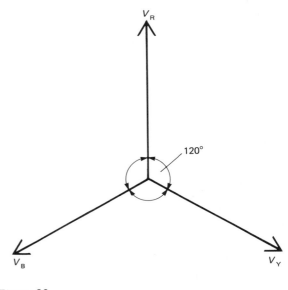

Figure 82

Solution

See Figure 83.

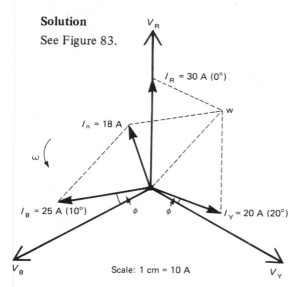

Figure 83

Note The solution requires the construction of two parallelograms. These are drawn between I_R and I_Y to give 'w' (the resultant) and between I_B and 'w' to give the second resultant I_n, (the current required in the neutral) i.e. 18 A. Figure 83 is not drawn to scale.

Part II students are expected to know trigonometry and as an exercise, the above solution can be solved using this method. It requires the finding of the resultant horizontal component and resultant vertical component of the phasor, then application of Pythagoras to find the neutral current. This is carried out in the next question.

145 With regard to the above question, find the neutral current by calculation.

Solution

The resultant horizontal component is given by:

$$I_Y \cos 10° - I_B \cos 20°$$
$$= (20 \times 0.984\,8) - (25 \times 0.939\,7)$$
$$= -3.7965 \text{ A}$$

Note the minus sign is only of directional importance.
The resultant vertical component is given by:

$$I_R - I_Y \sin 10° - I_B \sin 20°$$

$$= 30 - (20 \times 0.1736) - (25 \times 0.3420)$$

$$= 17.978 \text{ A}$$

Thus $I_n = \sqrt{-3.796\,5^2 + 17.978^2}$

$$= \mathbf{18.37 \text{ A}}$$

Note In case the angles of 10° and 20° cause confusion in the vertical component calculation, it should be pointed out that while I_Y leads its voltage by 20°, it is 10° from the reference line. Similarly, I_B lags its voltage by 10° but is 20° from the reference line.

146 An auto-transformer for single-phase operation has 600 turns. The primary supply of 240 V is connected to 450 turns while the secondary load is connected at 300 turns.
  (a) Show a diagram of the arrangement.
  (b) Determine the secondary voltage.
  (c) Ignoring losses, if the secondary load current is 10 A what current is taken from the supply?
  (d) What is the value of current in the common section of the transformer?

Solution

(a) See Figure 84.

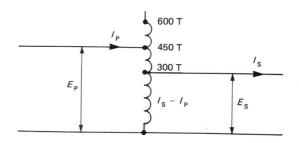

Figure 84

(b) $E_s = E_p \times \dfrac{N_s}{N_p}$

$$= 240 \times \frac{300}{450}$$

$$= \mathbf{160 \text{ V}}$$

(c) $I_p = \dfrac{N_s I_s}{N_p}$

$$= \frac{300 \times 10}{450}$$

$$= \mathbf{6.66 \text{ A}}$$

(d) Current in common section is:

$$I_s - I_p = 10 - 6.66 = \mathbf{3.34 \text{ A}}$$

147 In a 415 V/50 Hz, 3-phase, 4-wire supply
system, the following loads are connected:
  (a) one 50 Ω non-inductive load resistor
        across the red phase
  (b) one 1 000 W load having a p.f. of 0.8
        lagging across the yellow phase
  (c) one capacitive and resistive load of
        20 Ω reactance and 40 Ω resistance in
        series with each other across the blue
        phase
Find the phase currents in the system.

Solution

(a) Since $V_P = \dfrac{V_L}{\sqrt{3}}$ for a star connected

  system having a neutral, then:

$$V_P = \frac{415}{\sqrt{3}} = \textbf{240 V}$$

and:

$$I_L = I_p = \frac{V_P}{R} = \frac{240}{50} = \textbf{4.8 A}$$

(b) Since $P = V_P I_P \cos\phi$, then:

$$I_p = \frac{P}{V_P \times \cos\phi}$$

$$= \frac{1\ 000}{240 \times 0.8}$$

$$= \textbf{5.21 A}$$

(c) Since $Z = \sqrt{R^2 + X^2}$

$$= \sqrt{20^2 + 40^2}$$

$$= \textbf{44.72 Ω}$$

then:

$$I_P = \frac{V_P}{Z} = \frac{240}{44.72} = \textbf{5.37 A}$$

148 Figure 85 shows the layout of a 240 V/30 A
ring circuit with loads being taken off at points
B, C and D. Given the resistance of each section
to be: AB = 0.09 Ω, BC = 0.07 Ω, CD = 0.06 Ω
and DA = 0.08 Ω, find:
  (a) the current in each section of the ring and
        its direction
  (b) the voltages at each load point.

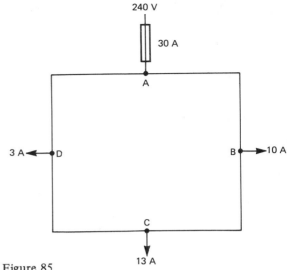

Figure 85

Solution

First, let the current in each section be as
follows:
  between AB it is I
  between BC it is I − 10
  between CD it is I − 23
  between DA it is I − 26
  Second, since the circuit is a ring circuit the
sum of the p.d.s. is zero.
Thus:

$$0.09I + 0.07(I - 10) + 0.06(I - 23)$$
$$+ 0.08(I - 26) = 0$$

Then:

$$0.09I + 0.07I + 0.06I + 0.08I$$
$$= 0.7 + 1.38 + 2.08$$

$$0.3I = 4.16$$

$$I = 13.87 \text{ A}$$

(a) Current in each section is as follows:

  From AB   I = **13.87 A**
  From BC   13.87 − 10 = **3.87 A**
  From CD   13.87 − 23 = **−9.13 A**
        (i.e. it flows from D to C)
  From DA   13.87 − 26 = **−12.13 A**
        (i.e. it flows from A to D)

(b) The voltage at B is:

$$240 - (13.87 \times 0.09) = \textbf{238.75 V}$$

The voltage at C is:

$$238.75 - (3.87 \times 0.07) = \mathbf{238.48\ V}$$

The voltage at D is:

$$240 - (12.13 \times 0.08) = \mathbf{239\ V}$$

149 A coil of copper wire has a resistance of 300 ohms at a temperature of 90 °C. Determine its resistance at a room temperature of 20 °C. Take the temperature coefficient of resistance of copper to be 0.004 3 Ω/Ω°C at 0 °C.

Solution

The formula to use in solving this problem is:

$$\frac{R_1}{R_2} = \frac{1 + \alpha t_1}{1 + \alpha t_2}$$

where $R_1 = 300\ \Omega$
$\quad\quad t_1 = 90\ °C$
$\quad\quad t_2 = 20\ °C$

By transposition:

$$R_2 = \left(\frac{1 + \alpha t_2}{1 + \alpha t_1}\right) R_1$$

$$= \left(\frac{1 + 0.086}{1 + 0.387}\right) \times 300$$

$$= \mathbf{234.9\ \Omega}$$

150 Draw a circuit diagram showing how an ammeter and selector switch are connected via current transformers in a 3-phase, 3-wire system in order for the ammeter to measure current in any line.

Solution

See Figure 86.

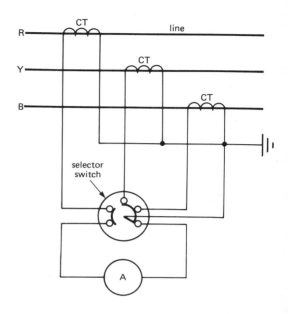

Figure 86

Note It should be pointed out that it is possible for a dangerously high voltage to be induced in the secondary winding of a current transformer if its circuit is left open. In view of this, the selector switch must be capable of shorting out those current transformers not in use in Figure 86.

Installation theory

Note Questions 151—92 are extracted from *Electrical Installation Technology 2.* Questions 193—200 are additional, based on the course syllabus.

---

151 Give a meaning for the following terms:
  (a) accessory
  (b) ambient temperature
  (c) bonded
  (d) extraneous conductive part
  (e) prospective short circuit current
                    Ex.1/Q1/Vol.2

Solution

  (a) An accessory can be any device connected with wiring and current-using appliances such as plugs and socket outlets but excludes electrical equipment such as a luminaire or motor.
  (b) This is the temperature of the air or other medium where equipment is to be used.
  (c) This is a term associated with items of metalwork for connection electrically to ensure a common potential exists. A bonding conductor is used for this purpose.
  (d) This is a conductive part which is liable to transmit a potential including earth potential but not itself forming part of the electrical installation.
  (e) This is the term given to explain the magnitude of the fault current that may be likely to flow under extreme short circuit conditions.

152 What precautions should be taken when:
  (a) handling heavy equipment
  (b) carrying a ladder and then erecting it in position
  (c) working with oily or greasy materials
  (d) drilling holes with a portable electric drill
  (e) terminating electrical conductors inside switchgear
                    Ex.1/Q2/Vol.2

Solution

Some precautions are as follows:
  (a) Try to seek assistance
      Use appropriate lifting tackle
      Wear appropriate clothing — protective gloves and shoes
      Be aware of other people around you and take care not to damage things in transit
  (b) Carry ladder with front elevated
      Stand ladder on firm base and use 4:1 rule for climbing
      Lash ladder at top or secure the bottom
      Only one person should be on a ladder and it is dangerous to over-reach
  (c) Use barrier cream on hands
      Be aware of the material slipping from grasp
      Wipe tools clean of oil or grease before use

(d)   Do not exert additional pressure on drill
       Keep lead away from the drilling area
       Be aware of the drill bit as it pierces the
            hole, scattering hot metal fragments.
       Keep drill straight
       Clean up area where drilling took place
(e)   Allow sufficient tails for terminating
       Avoid stress on conductors
       Check insulation for damage
       Tighten terminals and label conductors.

153   What is meant by the *earth-fault-loop path*?
       Draw a diagram of the path and indicate with
       arrows the route taken by the fault current.
                                    Ex.1/Q3/Vol.2

Solution

The *earth-fault-loop path* is the path taken by
escaping current to earth, i.e. earth-leakage
current. In Appendix 15 of the IEE Wiring
Regulations, the earth fault current loop starting
at the point of fault from the *phase* conductor
to earth, passes current into the circuit protective conductor, main earthing terminal and
earthing conductor then through the metallic
return path of the system (for TN systems) or
general mass of earth (for TT and IT systems).
The escaping current then passes through the
earthed neutral point of the supply transformer
and into the faulty phase back to the point of
fault. The opposition to this current is known
as the *earth-fault-loop impedance* (Z_S).
See Figure 87.

154   You have been called out to see why a motor
       is not running. The motor is a three-phase
       induction motor fed from a distribution board
       having its own main switch and direct-on-line
       starter. What procedure would you take to find
       the fault?   Ex.1/Q5/Vol.2

Solution

There may be variations to this solution since
the question does not give any indication
about the motor's condition — it may not be
running for a number of reasons. Suggestions
are:

1   Check rotor is free to rotate — remove belt
     or coupling
2   Check for overloading — remove load and
     check voltage
3   Test voltage while attempting to start
     motor — check for volt drop and single-
     phasing. The motor may make a humming
     noise
4   Trace fault back to starter, distribution
     board, main switch
5   Check correct fuse sizes, starter overloads,
     main switch blade action for high resistance
     contact
6   Test motor stator windings for any defects

155   From Figure 88, make a list of all electrical
       equipment required.   Ex.2/Q1/Vol.2

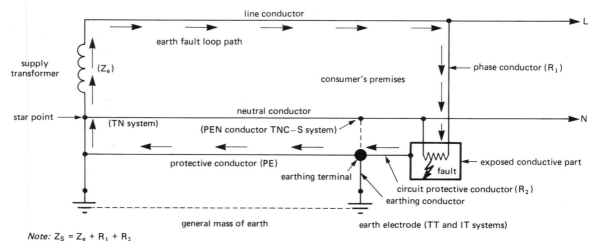

Note: $Z_S = Z_e + R_1 + R_2$

Figure 87

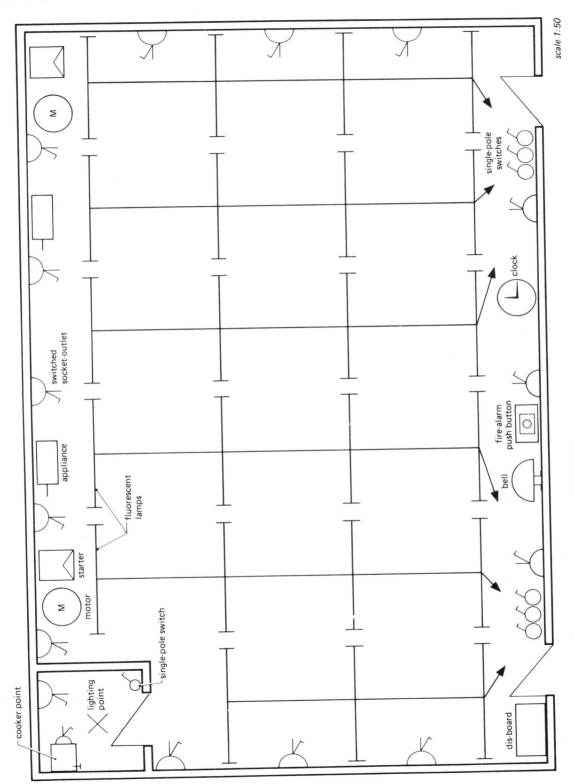

scale 1:50

single-pole switches

clock

fire-alarm push button

bell

dis-board

single-pole switch

lighting point

cooker point

motor

starter

fluorescent lamps

appliance

switched socket-outlet

Figure 88 *Layout drawing showing electrical requirements*

Solution

See Table 1.

Table 1

Qty.	Description	Cat. no.	Price
23	Fluorescent luminaires	Thorn PP40	
15	13 A switched socket outlets	MK 2977 ALM	
1	Distribution board	Wylex HS91	
1	Metalclad cooker control point	MK 5001	
1	1-Gang, 1-way s.p. switch	MK 3591 ALM	
2	3-Gang, 1-way s.p. switch assembly	MK 892 ALM (complete)	
1	Dome bell	Gent 500AC	
1	Fire alarm point	Gent 1102	
2	Redring fan heaters	50–811103	
1	Batternholder	MK 1173 WHI	
2	Memdol single-phase a.c. motor switches	MEM 2 SPS + 24 SPH	
2	Brook Crompton Parkinson Motors		
1	Fused connector box for electric clock	MK 993 WHI	
1	Tann Synchronome clock		

156 Describe in your own words the procedure taken to rescue a person receiving an electric shock from a portable drill.   Ex.1/Q4/Vol.2

Solution

See Question 58, page 35. In view of the nature of the accident, it is important that an accident form be completed and that the area is cordoned off for investigation. See Question 62, page 37, for the completion of an accident form.

157 Draw block and circuit diagrams of the control-gear for a 3-phase induction motor. State on the diagrams the size of cable and fuse protection assuming the motor will take a current of 15 A.   Ex.2/Q2/Vol.2

Solution

See Figure 89.

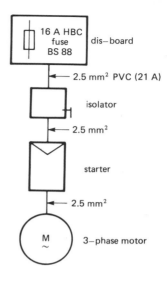

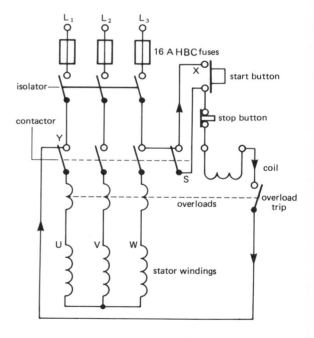

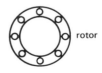

Figure 89

158 Draw a circuit diagram of the lighting control switching illustrated in Figure 90.

Ex.2/Q3/Vol.2

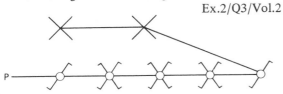

Figure 90

Solution

See Figure 91.

159 Show an exploded view of a 3-core MIMS screw-on seal termination. Label all parts.

Ex.2/Q4/Vol.2

Solution

See Figure 92.

160 From relevant manufacturers' catalogues, select products for the following items, quoting the catalogue number where applicable:

(a)   13 A switched socket outlet
(b)   5 A single-pole, one-way switch
(c)   60 A, 8-way metalclad consumer unit
(d)   MCBs—two 5 A, one 15 A, one 20 A, two 30 A and two blank shields
(e)   85 W (1800 mm) single fluorescent luminaire (with diffuser)

Ex.2/Q5/Vol.2

Solution

(a)   Crabtree 2214 QG
(b)   MK 3591 ALM
(c)   Crabtree 708/2
(d)   Two 50/05; one 50/15; one 50/20; two 50/30 and two 743 blank plates
(e)   Thorn PPQ 675 plus PPC6

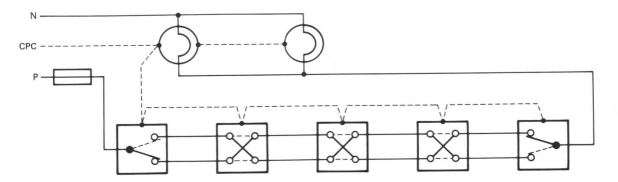

Figure 91

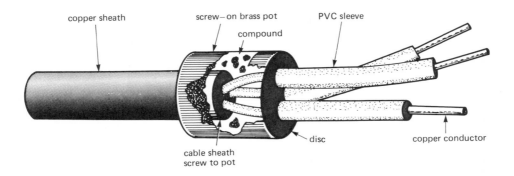

Figure 92

161 Reproduce the outline of Figure 88 on an overlay and show the conduit routes and cables (sizes and numbers in various sections) for the lighting installations taken back to the distribution board.   Ex.2/Q6/Vol.2

Solution

See Figure 93.

162 Draw a bar chart of a simple project involving electrical work only.   Ex.2/Q7/Vol.2

Solution

The solution to this question is based upon Figure 94 (see Figure 19 on page 25 of *Electrical Installation Technology 2*). The activities for the network are as follows:

0–1	Erection of site hut ($\frac{1}{2}$)
1–2	Study of drawings and site ($\frac{1}{2}$)
2–3	Start erecting conduit (1)
2–4	Start erecting switchgear (2)
3–6	Continue conduit installation (6)
3–9	Wire conduit system (5)
4–5	Install sub-main cables (3)
4–8	Erect trunking system (6)
5–11	Install disboard cables (8)
6–7	Terminate conduits to machines (1)
7–11	Wire and connect machines (3)
8–10	Wire trunking system ($\frac{1}{2}$)
8–12	Install machines (8)
9–14	Connect lighting installation (10)
10–13	Label disboards and machines (1)
11–14	Wire disboards (2)
12–15	Test and commission machines (8)
13–15	Test and commission lighting (3)
14–15	Clear site ($\frac{1}{2}$)
15–16	Handover electrical installation ($\frac{1}{2}$)

Note Figures in brackets are times measured in days.

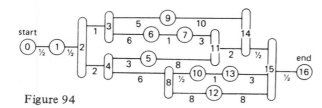

Figure 94

Figure 95 overleaf is a bar chart for the project. The dotted line illustrates those activities taking the longest time to complete the project.

163 Prepare notes on the following topics:
(a) clocking on and off routines
(b) tea and meal breaks
(c) washing and changing facilities
(d) site meetings   Ex.2/Q8/Vol.2

Solution

(a) This method of time-keeping lends itself favourably to employers who have a large workforce, where accurate time-keeping is essential to encourage punctuality. The system often preferred is the punch card method which takes a relatively short time to carry out and provides the employer with immediate information of employees' time-keeping to work out wages.

In service industries like the electrical contracting industry, the punch card system might be difficult to operate, mainly because of contracts worked away from the office and overtime working. In such circumstances, a good chargehand or foreman is all that is required to organize a small workforce.

(b) These are taken at set times laid down by the employer. Meal breaks including washing time are generally of one hour duration and are unpaid, whereas tea-breaks which are usually of ten/fifteen minute periods in the morning and afternoon are paid by the employer.

It is in the interest of the employees not to exceed the times granted by their employers as this will only result in lost production time and lost profit for the employer and eventual unemployment for the employees.

(c) These facilities will be found on the premises of the work place. They may be provided by the employer in a site hut or cabin or provided by a main builder

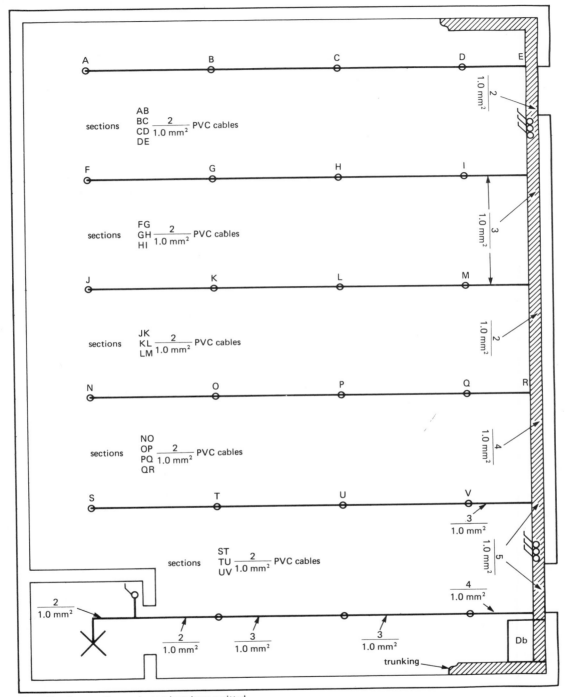

Note: Circuit protective conductors have been omitted.

Figure 93

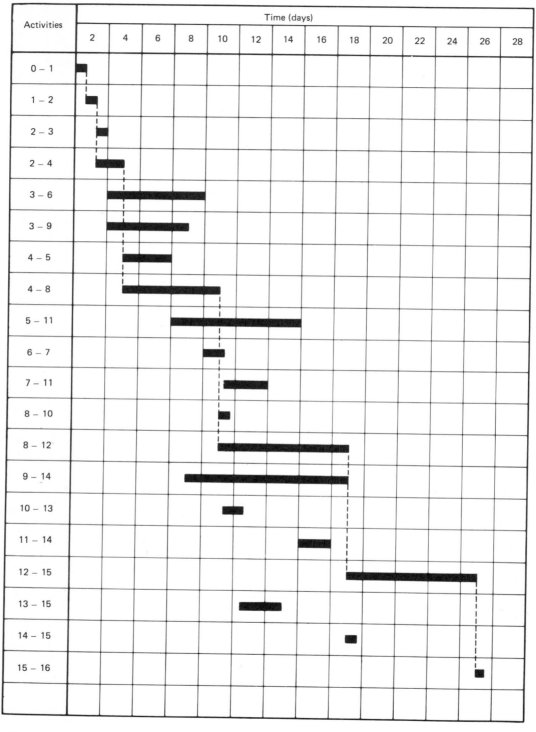

Figure 95

contractor or client as a shared facility. Such facilities will enable the employees to maintain a reasonable standard of hygiene at his/her place of work.

(d) These are usually arranged by the main builder of a large contract to discuss its progress/delay/alterations etc. The meetings bring together interested parties such as electricians, plumbers and carpenters etc. Generally it is the charge-hands and foremen of the respective trades who become involved and who have the opportunity to discuss their problems. Such meetings should aim to improve the relations between the different contractors and allow a free flow of work for ensuing weeks until the next meeting.

It is good practice to keep a record of the minutes of each meeting and for them to be agreed and signed before each new meeting commences.

164 What is meant by the following with regard to electrical contracting:
(a) contract
(b) specification
(c) variation order
(d) bills of quantities   Ex.2/Q9/Vol.2

Solution

(a) A contract is an agreement which contemplates and creates an obligation — see page 25 of *Electrical Installation Technology 2* for further details.
(b) This is a document which specifies the requirements for carrying out work — see page 25 of *Electrical Installation Technology 2* for further details.
(c) A variation order is an architect's instruction (AI) used for the purpose of carrying out changes or additions to work — see page 26 of *Electrical Installation Technology 2* for further details.
(d) A bill of quantities is a list of all the components of an installation which have been compiled by a quantity surveyor — see page 26 of *Electrical Installation Technology 2* for further details.

165 What is the function of the following bodies:
(a) trade union
(b) Joint Industrial Board (JIB)
(c) Advisory, Conciliation and Arbitration Service (ACAS)   Ex.2/Q10/Vol.2

Solution

The answer to this question can be found on page 27 of *Electrical Installation Technology 2* under the heading '*Industrial relations*'. Briefly:

(a) A trade union ensures that its members are provided with a reasonable standard of wages and conditions at work and sees that its members are not victimized by employers.
(b) The JIB regulates the relations between employers and employees within the industry by providing benefits to those persons concerned for the purpose of stimulating and furthering the improvement of the industry.
(c) ACAS arbitrates impartially in decisions between employers and unions where talks on work matters have previously broken down.

166 Show the circuit wiring of a domestic consumer's installation comprising the following circuits:
(a) upstairs and downstairs lighting on separate circuits
(b) immersion heater circuit (night supply)
(c) cooker circuit
(d) two ring circuits
(e) storage heater circuit   Ex.3/Q1/Vol.2

Solution

See Figure 96.

167 Select an appropriate cable size from the Tables of the IEE Wiring Regulations for a circuit having the following details:
(a) PVC single-core cables in conduit
(b) load — single-phase 240 V taking 30 A
(c) ambient temperature 30 °C
(d) length of run 43 m

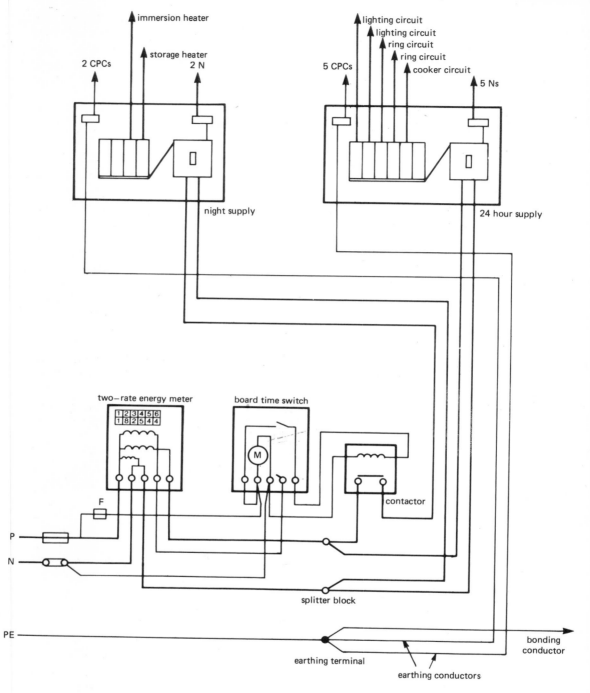

Figure 96

(e)   overload protection is by m.c.b.
(f)   conduit already contains five single-
      phase circuits   Ex.3/Q2/Vol.2

Solution

The procedure is as follows:
(i)   Design current of circuit = 30 A
(ii)   Protective m.c.b. rated at 30 A. (see
       Table 41A2 of the IEE Wiring Regula-
       tions)
(iii) Select appropriate Table from IEE
       Regulations, i.e. Table 9D1, columns 2
       and 3. Follow procedure in Appendix 9,
       (4(i)). Correction factor for ambient
       temperature does not apply. Correction
       factor for grouping is 0.55 (see Table 9B).
(iv)   Select cable from Table 9D1 which can
       carry a current equal to or greater than:

$$\frac{30}{0.55} = 54.5 \text{ A}$$

Cable chosen is 10 mm^2 with current
carrying capacity of 55 A.
(v)   Check volt drop to see if it is less than the
       permissible volt drop allowed, i.e. 2.5%
       of 240 V = 6 V.
       Volt drop = 43 × 30 × 0.004 2 = 5.42 V
       The above cable is suitable for the load.

Note   The question assumes the conduit does not
contain any circuit protective conductors.

168   In the process of calculating the loading on the
main cable of a hotel installation, a diversity on
cooking appliances was applied. From Table 4B,
Appendix 4 of the IEE Wiring Regulations,
determine the loading for five cookers each
rated at 15 kW, 240 V.   Ex.3/Q3/Vol.2

Solution

Current loading of one appliance is:

$$I = \frac{P}{V} = \frac{15\ 000}{240} = 62.5 \text{ A}$$

From Table 4B the allowance is 100% f.l. of
largest appliance, 80% f.l. of second largest
appliance and 60% f.l. of remaining appliances.
Thus the assessed current demand is:

$$62.5 + (0.8 \times 62.5) + (0.6 \times 62.5 \times 3) = 224.5 \text{ A}$$

The hotel would probably be supplied with
3-phases, 4-wire in which case the cookers
would be balanced across the phases with other
loadings.

169   What is meant by:
(a)   protective conductor
(b)   growth factor
(c)   ambient temperature
(d)   diversity allowance   Ex.3/Q4/Vol.2

Solution

The answer to these terms can be found in both
Electrical Installation Technology 1 and *2* and
the IEE Wiring Regulations.
(a)   This is a conductor used to protect against
      the likelihood of electric shock. It con-
      nects together exposed conductive parts,
      extraneous conductive parts, the main
      earthing terminal, earth electrode and
      earthed point of source.
(b)   This is a factor which considers the like-
      lihood of future loadings on switchgear
      and cables.
(c)   This is the temperature of the air or other
      medium where the equipment is to be
      used.
(d)   This is a ratio of minimum actual loading
      and installed loading based on the assump-
      tion that all equipment in an installation
      will not be in full use at any one time.

170   What are the advantages and disadvantages of
the following systems:
(a)   ring main system
(b)   rising main system
(c)   TN–C–S system   Ex.3/Q5/Vol.2

Solution

(a)   The most important advantage of this
      system is that load points are fed two
      ways making full use of conductor c.s.a. as
      a result of diversity applied to the load
      points. Other advantages allow break-
      downs on the system easier to trace while
      still retaining continuity of supply else-
      where as well as isolation of part of the

system for maintenance purposes. Volt drop problems are also reduced.

There are few disadvantages with a ring main but one cannot ignore the increased cost of cable and duplication of switchgear for isolation purposes. The system is also limited: its greatest use is on primary supply distribution systems.

(b)   This is another form of main supply system which lends itself to multi-storey type buildings where lateral supplies are tapped off to feed floors. Systems are available up to 2 000 A using high conductivity copper busbars; this rating and flexibility of supply are seen as its greatest advantages.

Expense may be seen as its greatest disadvantage and this may limit its choice to the types of building mentioned.

(c)   The main advantage with this supply system is the reduced cost to the supply authority in terms of cable cores and termination methods on distributor cables. The system is known as p.m.e. where the neutral and protective faults are converted into phase to earth faults.

The main disadvantage of the system is that if the PEN conductor becomes an open circuit, it results in a possible danger to consumers.

171   Draw a diagram of the intake position of a consumer's premises supplied for p.m.e. connection. Show also the concentric service cable joined to the cut-outs, the meter connection, fuseboard connections and bonding arrangements.   Ex.3/Q6/Vol.2

Solution

See Figure 97.

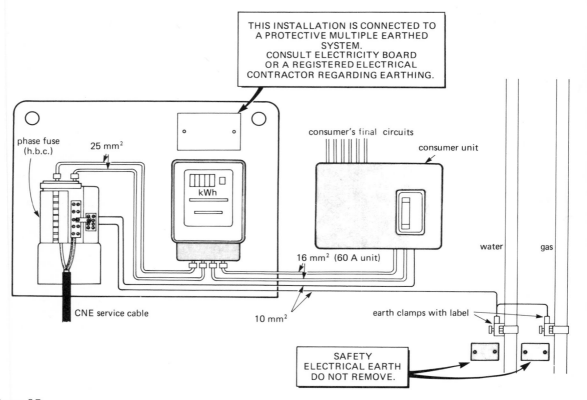

Figure 97

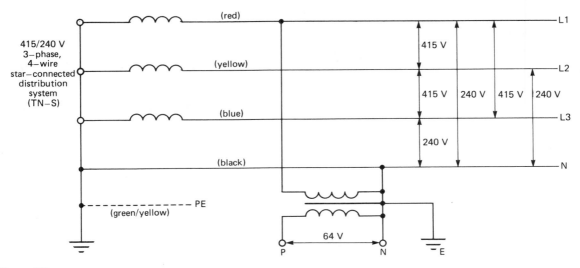

Figure 98

172 Determine the size of cable trunking for the following conductor numbers and sizes:
(a) fifteen 1.5 mm²
(b) twenty 2.5 mm²
(c) six 4.0 mm²
Assume all are stranded PVC single-core cables. Refer to Appendix 12 of the IEE Wiring Regulations. Ex.3/Q7/Vol.2

Solution

This is a straightforward question and should present no difficulty. Reference should be made to Table 12E and 12 F. In Table 12E, 1.5 mm² has a factor of 8.1; 2.5 mm² has a factor of 11.4, and 4.0 mm² a factor of 15.2. Thus:

total cable factor = (8.1 × 15) + (11.4 × 20)
                                    + (15.2 × 6)

= 440.7

Referring to Table 12F, the nearest size trunking is 75 × 25 mm having a factor of 738.

173 Draw a 415 V/240 V distribution system and indicate on the drawing both line and phase voltages between red, yellow and blue lines and between each phase and neutral. Show also, how 64 V can be obtained through a double-wound transformer. Ex.3/Q8/Vol.2

Solution

See Figure 98.

Note It is possible to obtain 64 V from a 110 V, 3-phase, 4-wire supply system.

174 What are the IEE Wiring Regulations covering motor circuits? Ex.5/Q6/Vol.2

Solution

Reference should be made to Chapter 55, Section 552. Equipment and cables feeding motors should be rated to carry the full load current of the motors. The supply undertaking should be consulted regarding starting arrangements for those motors requiring heavy starting currents. Motors exceeding 0.37 kW require control equipment incorporating means of protection against overcurrent, although if a motor is part of some current-using equipment complying with a British Standard as a whole, it is exempt from such protection.

Every electric motor must be provided with a means to prevent automatic restarting which could cause a danger. The provision of *no-volt protection* in the starter/control equipment may meet this requirement. Where a motor is started and stopped at intervals by an automatic control device, the requirements do not apply, providing other adequate measures are taken against danger of unexpected restarting.

175 Explain the procedure you would take in testing a three-phase, six-terminal cage induction motor for:
(a)   winding continuity
(b)   winding insulation resistance
(c)   reversal of direction   Ex.5/Q7/Vol.2

Solution

(a)   When testing a motor's windings for continuity, all windings must be disconnected from each other. Often a multirange ohmmeter is used and all three windings should give the same ohmic values. It is important for the winding ends to be marked or labelled in case reverse phasing of one winding occurs — this would make the motor run roughly and it would not take load.

(b)   In practice, the insulation resistance to earth of a motor's winding should not be

less than 1 megohm. This test is carried out using an insulation resistance tester which has 500 V/1 000 V selection and is capable of measuring high ohmic values. The windings can be tested separately to earth or when connected together and tested to earth.

(c)   The first thing to observe is the direction the motor is running. It is important to check that no harm will occur with its connected load after reversal. Disconnect motor from load if in any doubt. Reversal is achieved by changing over any two supply leads on the motor.

176 Draw a diagram of a single-phase a.c. motor controlled by a direct-on-line contactor starter having thermal overloads. The circuit should include remote start and stop buttons.
                                                              Ex.5/Q8/Vol.2

Solution

See Figure 99.

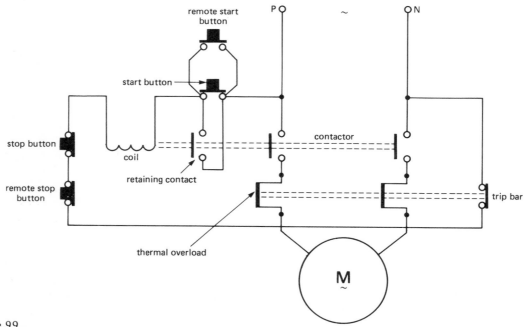

Figure 99

177 (a) Explain the meaning of *stroboscopic effect*. Why is the condition dangerous in some instances?

(b) Show by means of a diagram how twelve fluorescent lamps can be arranged to minimize the above effect.

Ex.6/Q1/Vol.2

Solution

(a) Stroboscopic effect is a phenomenon peculiar to discharge lighting since the a.c. supply passes through zero twice every cycle. This causes the light to flicker at twice the supply frequency and while not noticeable to the eye the effect can make rotating objects look stationary and create a dangerous situation.

In practice, fluorescent tubes produce an 'after-glow' effect which eliminates the problem. Also luminaires can be wired as lead-lag circuits. The method shown in Figure 100 is to arrange the tubes on different phases but this can only be achieved if a 3-phase supply is available.

(b) See Figure 100.

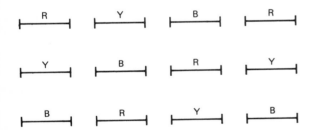

Figure 100

178 What is meant by the following terms:
(a) efficacy
(b) luminous flux
(c) illuminance
(d) utilization factor
(e) maintenance factor   Ex.6/Q2/Vol.2

Solution

(a) *Efficacy* is the term expressing the ratio of luminous flux and power consumed of a lamp.

(b) *Luminous flux* is the flow of light sent out by a light source, it is measured in lumens. There are 4 lumens emitted by a point source of 1 candela.

(c) *Illuminance* is the amount of light in lumens falling on unit area, 1m/m^2.

(d) *Utilization factor* is a term that shows the light reaching the working plane is reduced so that the power of the light source will have to be increased to obtain the desired illuminance. As a coefficient it expresses the ratio of light flux falling on the working plane and total light flux produced by all light sources.

(e) *Maintenance factor* is expressed as a ratio of illumination from a dirty installation to that from the same installation when clean. The factor allows for dust accumulation on luminaires, ageing of light source and deterioration of decor.

179 Draw a circuit diagram of a high pressure sodium vapour discharge lamp and explain the function of its controlgear. Also describe its colour appearance, efficacy and two typical uses.   Ex.6/Q3/Vol.2

Solution

See Figure 80 which shows the controlgear and circuitry for a SON lamp. The *ballast* for such a lamp is housed in a container filled with polyester to enable it to withstand a long life. The main function of the ballast is to limit current through the lamp and also provide the lamp with the correct voltage. Some wattage lamps require three ballasts for this requirement.

In order for the lamp to light, a series of high voltage pulses is applied by an *ignitor*. These pulses are of very short duration and because of capacitive attenuation the length of cable between the ignitor and the lamp is limited. For example, the maximum length of cable between lamp and ignitor for a 400 W SON lamp is 17 m. When the lamp is struck the ignitor ceases to function. The lamp takes several minutes to reach full brightness but because the sodium vapour pressure in the arc tube builds up to several atmospheres, the lamp cannot restrike immediately after being switched off — it needs to cool down first.

In terms of colour appearance, SON lamps emit a pleasant golden white light with reasonable colour rendering, so that colours are distinguishable. The efficacy is quite high, for a 400 W lamp with lighting design lumens of 44 000 lm it is 110 lm/w. Two typical uses for the lamp are: (a) sport centres — swimming pools, gymnasiums etc. (b) floodlighting.

180 Six 125 W, 240 V fluorescent discharge lamps are to be connected into a lighting distribution fuseboard. Determine:
(a)   the load current of the circuit (assuming the 1.8 factor)
(b)   the size of fuse protecting the circuit
(c)   the current rating of the control circuit switches   Ex.6/Q4/Vol.2

Solution

(a) $I = \dfrac{P \times 1.8}{V}$

$ = \dfrac{125 \times 6 \times 1.8}{240}$

$ = \textbf{5.6 A}$ (approx.)

(b)   Size of fuse (BS 3036) is **15 A**

(c)   Current rating of control switches is **15—20 A**. See Regulation 537—19 (switches for discharge lighting circuits)

181 What are the IEE Wiring Regulations (15th Edition) with regard to:
(a)   provision of a fireman's emergency switch controlling a high voltage neon sign
(b)   wiring of capacitors
(c)   luminaires
(d)   ceiling roses   Ex.6/Q5/Vol.2

Solution

(a)   Reference should be made to Regulations 476—12 and 476—13. The former regulation deals with unattended interior installations and exterior installations, both operating above low voltage. The latter regulation concerns the provision of the switch: in exterior installations it should be adjacent to the discharge sign, or a notice indicating the position of the switch should be adjacent to the sign. For interior installations, the switch has to be located in the main entrance or position agreed with by the local fire authority. In both cases, the switch height must not exceed 2.75 m from the ground and where more than one switch is installed on any one building, each switch has to be clearly labelled to indicate what it controls. The fire authority needs to be notified of this.

(b)   Regulation 461—4 states that means shall be provided for the discharge of capacitive electrical energy. The notes in Regs. 512—1 and 512—2 refer to the adequacy of switches and circuit breakers of capacitive equipment, and Regulation 554—5 states that ancillary equipment for discharge lighting installations, such as capacitors, shall be either totally enclosed in a substantially earthed metal container or placed in a suitably ventilated enclosure to BS 476 Part 5 or be of fire-resistant construction.

(c)   There are a number of requirements for luminaires and reference should be made to the index of the IEE Wiring Regulations. Some of these are:
(i)   In a bathroom it is recommended to use a totally enclosed luminaire (Reg. 471—38).
(ii)   All fixed luminaries are to be placed or guarded to prevent ignition of any materials placed in proximity to them or their lamps — guards which are used must be capable of withstanding the heat from the luminaire or lamp (Reg. 422—4).
(iii) Where a flexible cord supports a luminaire, the maximum mass supported by the cord must not exceed 2 kg for a 0.5 mm² cord,

3 kg for a 0.75 mm² cord and 5 kg for a 1.0 mm² cord (Reg. 524–32). Also see switching off for mechanical maintenance (Reg. 476–8), emergency switching (Reg. 476–13) and other requirements (Regs. 476–17 to 18).

(d) With regard to ceiling roses, see Regulation 412–6 (an exemption from the requirements to open an enclosure); Regulation 533–19 (must not be installed in any circuit operating above 250 V) and

Regulation 553–20 (unless specially designed they cannot be used for the attachment of more than one outgoing flexible cord).

182 Complete the wiring in Figure 101.

Ex.6/Q6/Vol.2

Solution

See Figure 102.

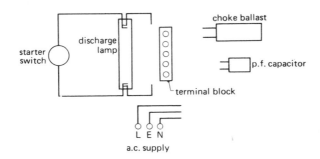

Figure 101

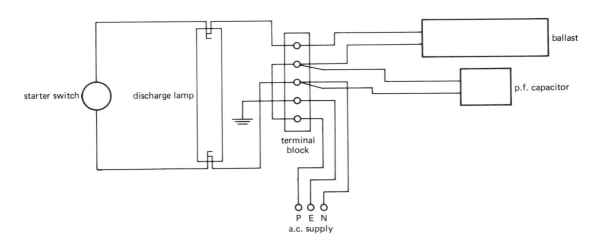

Figure 102

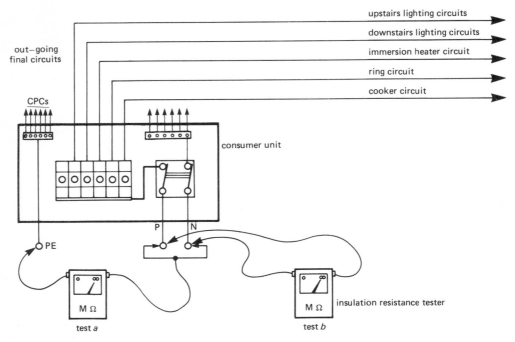

Figure 103

183 Draw a circuit diagram of a 6-way consumer
unit, showing meter tails and outgoing final
circuit wiring, and illustrate on the diagram the
method(s) of carrying out an insulation resistance test. State the required ohmic values of
the test(s).   Ex.7/Q1/Vol.2

Solution

See Figure 103. Reference should be made to
the IEE Wiring Regulations, Regs. 613—5,
613—6 and 613—7. Required ohmic value is
1 megohm for completed installation.

184 A factory's electrical installation wiring is
subdivided when given an insulation resistance
test. The various sections have readings of
40 MΩ, 20 MΩ, 1 MΩ, 100 MΩ and 5 MΩ.
What is the overall result of the test?
                              Ex.7/Q2/Vol.2
Solution

A similar question to this was asked in Question
93. If the test was made at the intake position,
the test instrument would read less than 1
megohm.

Since the sections are in parallel with each
other, then:

$$\frac{1}{R} = \frac{1}{40} + \frac{1}{20} + \frac{1}{1} + \frac{1}{100} + \frac{1}{5}$$

$$= 0.025 + 0.05 + 1 + 0.01 + 0.2$$

$$= 1.285 \ \Omega$$

Thus:

$$\frac{R}{1} = \frac{1}{1.285} = \mathbf{0.778 \ \Omega}$$

185 Draw a circuit diagram of a test on a fault
voltage operated earth leakage circuit breaker
as required by the IEE Wiring Regulations.
                              Ex.7/Q3/Vol.2
Solution

The answer to this question has already been
given — see Figure 39, Question 85.

186 Determine the maximum permitted earth
fault loop impedances for the following final
circuits:

(a) A 240 V immersion heater protected by a 15 A semi-enclosed fuse (BS 3036). See Table 41A2(c) of the IEE Wiring Regulations. What current is likely to flow to rupture the fuse?

(b) A 240 V motor protected by a 32 A h.b.c. fuse (BS 88). See Table 41A2(a) of the IEE Wiring Regulations. What current is likely to flow to rupture the fuse?

(c) A 240 V automatic control circuit protected by a 10 A circuit breaker (BS 3871 Type 2). See Table 41A2(e) of the IEE Wiring Regulations. What current is likely to flow to trip the circuit breaker?

Ex.7/Q4/Vol.2

Solution

(a) An immersion heater is a fixed piece of equipment and Regulation 413−4 (ii) requires a circuit disconnection within 5 seconds. From Table 41A2(c), the maximum earth fault impedance is 5.6 ohms. At this impedance the fault current would be:

$$I_F = \frac{V_P}{Z_S}$$

where V_P is the phase voltage
Z_S is the loop impedance

Thus $I_F = \frac{240}{5.6} = $ **42.9 A** (approx.)

Note A semi-enclosed fuse normally ruptures at about twice its current rating. See Figure 11 IEE Wiring Regulations and determine disconnection time.

(b) The motor is regarded as fixed equipment and it will be seen from the appropriate Table that its maximum earth loop impedance is 1.8 ohms. Under these conditions the fault current would be:

$$I_F = \frac{240}{1.8} = \textbf{133.3 A}$$

See Figure 8 of IEE Regulations and check disconnection time.

(c) This circuit is also seen as fixed equipment and from the Table the maximum earth loop impedance is 3.4 ohms. Under

these conditions the fault current would be:

$$I_F = \frac{240}{3.4} = \textbf{71 A}$$

See Figure 14 of the IEE Regulations and check disconnection time.

187 What are the IEE Wiring Regulations requirements covering the issuing of:
(a) completion certificate
(b) inspection certificate   Ex.7/Q5/Vol.2

Solution

(a) When inspection and testing work of an electrical installation has been carried out, the electrical contractor or installer is required to give a completion certificate to the person ordering the work. The form is set out in Appendix 16 of the IEE Regulations and any defects or omissions revealed are to be made good before the certificate is given. This requirement applies to all work including alterations to existing installations. Here the contractor or installer has to report to the person ordering the work, any defects found in related parts of the existing installation.

(b) An inspection certificate must be attached to every completion certificate. The certificate is shown in Appendix 16. It lists many items of inspection and testing and again, has to be given by the contractor or installer to the person ordering the test. It is recommended that inspections of installations be carried out every five years or less. Any poor test results must be reported on this certificate. Both certificates are required to be signed.

188 Draw a circuit diagram of six 13 A single socket outlets connected in the form of a ring final circuit fed from a consumer unit. Illustrate on the diagram a method of testing ring circuit continuity. Explain how you would test socket outlets connected by means of spurs.

Ex.7/Q6/Vol.2

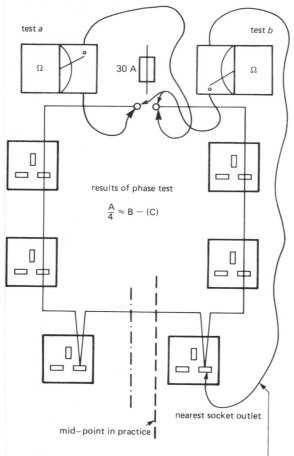

results of phase test

$$\frac{A}{4} \approx B - (C)$$

nearest socket outlet

mid—point in practice

Figure 104

test lead of known resistance (C)

Solution

See Figure 104. Socket outlets on spurs are radial circuits. There are no specified test requirements. However, if a test does have to be made, the socket outlet connecting the spur can have its live conductors, in turn, shorted to earth. While at the origin of the spur, a test with an ohmmeter to find the earthed conductor(s) is made.

189 Describe a test to determine the value of earth loop impedance of an earthed concentric wiring system and state what precautions must be taken when carrying out the test.

Ex.7/Q7/Vol.2

Solution

An earthed concentric wiring system is a TN–C system in which the PEN conductor is the sheath of the cable – see Figure 3, Appendix 3, IEE Wiring Regulations. A number of the regulations are applicable to PEN conductors – see Section 546 and note below.

In practice there are two basic methods of testing for earth loop impedance (a) using a phase-earth loop tester and (b) using a neutral-earth loop tester. The latter method cannot be used on this wiring system since the earth and neutral are combined in one conductor.

The phase-earth loop test is made by injecting a current (of short duration) of about 20 A from the phase conductor to the PEN conductor. The fault current passes through a known resistor (about 10 ohm) and circulates through the earth fault loop. The value of current can either be measured directly with an ammeter in series with the resistor or using a ballistic instrument calibrated directly in ohms but actually reading the p.d. across the resistor.

As a precaution when making the test, it is advisable to check the PEN conductor first to see if there are any noticeable breaks. Such a break in the system would lead to full supply voltage appearing across the phase and PEN conductors on the test side of the fault.

Note This system is only permitted where the supply authorities agree. Otherwise it can only be used where the mains are taken through a transformer or converter in order to avoid the supply authority's metallic connection. Further approval of its use can be obtained for a private generating plant.

190 List the instruments for making the following tests:
(a)   verification of polarity on a live installation
(b)   earth electrode test
(c)   earth leakage circuit breaker test
(d)   earth fault loop impedance test

Ex.7/Q8/Vol.2

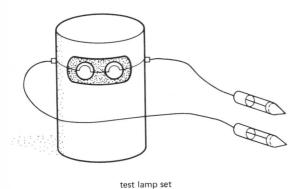

test lamp set

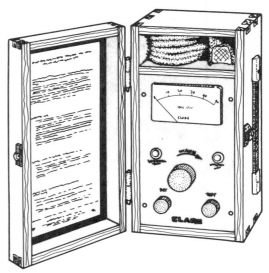

ELCB tester

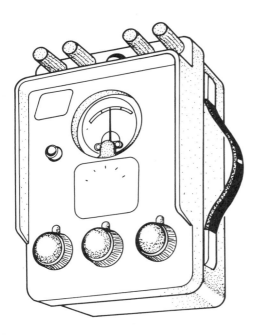

earth tester

Figure 105

Solution

(a)   test lamp set
(b)   null-balance earth tester
(c)   ELCB tester
(d)   impedance tester

These instruments are illustrated in Figure 105.

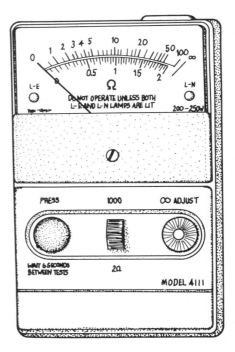

impedance tester

191 Explain how you would set about testing a three-phase motor's stator winding for (a) continuity and (b) insulation resistance.

Ex.7/Q9/Vol.2

Solution

The testing procedure is the same as that given in Question 175. First, the windings need to be disconnected from the supply and for continuity an ohmmeter is used. If the motor only has three winding ends brought out, test between separate pairs. All three readings should be the same. For insulation resistance, test the windings down to earth. The readings should be above 1 MΩ.

192 Explain the difference between insulation resistance and conductor continuity.

Ex.7/Q10/Vol.2

Solution

The difference between the two terms is that *insulation resistance* is concerned with the opposition of leakage current by the insulation medium of circuit cables and components of the wiring system whereas *conductor continuity* is concerned with the *soundness* of the conducting path taken by current as it flows through the circuit conductors.

Insulation resistance should have a very high ohmic value such that any leakage current which does flow from conductor to earth, does not exceed the mandatory limit of 1/10 000 part of the maximum current supplied to to the installation. The IEE Wiring Regulations require 1 MΩ to be obtained as the minimum insulation resistance value for a test on a completed installation. Insulation resistance of cables is inversely proportional to the length, whereas conductor resistance is proportional to length.

193 Regulation 413—4 of the IEE Wiring Regulations stipulates that the maximum disconnection time for final circuits supplying socket outlets is 0.4 seconds, whereas for final circuits supplying fixed equipment it is 5 seconds. Explain why this is so.

Solution

The Regulations recognize that when an earth fault occurs in an installation, the degree of risk is greater when using portable equipment which is gripped by the hands compared with equipment which is fixed. Also the degree of risk is greater if a person uses equipment outside the equipotential zone, i.e. the area where all exposed conductive and extraneous conductive parts are bonded together, for example, equipment used in the garden. For this reason, socket outlets supplying such equipment must be protected by a residual current device of 30 mA rating.

194 A 240 V/13 A socket outlet is wired in 2.5 mm^2 twin and earth PVC cable and protected by a 15 A fuse to BS 1361. If the protective conductor is 1.5 mm^2, determine the maximum length of circuit cable. Assume the impedance of the supply (Z_e) to be 1.2 ohms and the socket outlet complying with Reg. 413—4 of the IEE Wiring Regulations. The cable has copper conductors.

Solution

This question requires reference to the IEE Regulations.

First, find the value of maximum earth fault loop impedance from Table 41A1(b) for the fuse size given. Thus:

$$Z_S = 3.4 \ \Omega$$

Second, find $R_1 + R_2$ from the expression $Z_S = Z_e + R_1 + R_2$ (see page 127, Appendix 8, IEE Regulations. *Note* Appendix 8 is under review).

Thus: $Z_S - Z_e = R_1 + R_2$

$$3.4 - 1.2 = 2.2 \ \Omega$$

Note   The 2.2 Ω is the maximum value of phase conductor and protective conductor respectively.

Third, from Table 8D of the Regulations, since the protective conductor is 1.5 mm^2 the value of $R_1 + R_2$ per metre is 0.030 Ω/m. Thus, the maximum length of cable is:

$$\frac{2.2}{0.030} = 73.3 \text{ m}$$

195 Determine the maximum disconnection time for the following cables:
  (a) 50 mm² twin armoured cable with 90° thermosetting insulation and aluminium conductors
  (b) 50 mm² mineral-insulated cable with copper conductors
  (c) 50 mm² twin PVC insulated cable with copper conductors

Assume a prospective fault current or effective short circuit current of 4 000 A.

Solution

Reference should be made to the adiabatic equation on page 37 of the IEE Wiring Regulations. This equation is used when the cross-sectional area of conductors is 10 mm² or more and for short circuits of duration up to 5 seconds.

(a) $t = \dfrac{k^2S^2}{I^2}$

    $= \dfrac{94^2 \times 50^2}{4\,000^2} = 1.38$ s

(b) $t = \dfrac{135^2 \times 50^2}{4\,000^2} = 2.84$ s

(c) $t = \dfrac{115^2 \times 50^2}{4\,000^2} = 2.06$ s

196 (a) Show by means of a diagram how a standard 415 V, 3-phase 4-wire supply to a factory could be used to feed the following loads:
    (i) 240 V discharge lighting arranged so as to minimize stroboscopic effect

    (ii) one 415 V 3-phase motor
    (iii) two 415 V single phase welders
  (b) (i) state why balancing of loads is desirable
    (ii) state why a neutral is essential on the above three-phase supply

CGLI/II/83

Solution

(a) This part of the question requires diagrams of how the loads are divided over the 3-phase, 4-wire supply. For this see Figure 106.

(b) (i) It should be realized that a balanced system allows equal loading on each phase of the supply. By doing this the correct size switchgear and cables can be chosen. It would be a nonsense to have one phase taking a large load while the other two were taking small loads since selection of a main cable is based on the maximum design current of the system over the three phases. Two lightly loaded phases would be un-economical resulting in poor utilization.

    (ii) It is very difficult to balance a system completely because certain loads are running at different times to other loads. Lighting on one phase may be switched off and the welding plant on and off at different times. With the exception of the 3-phase motor the system above is unbalanced and it is the function of the neutral to take back to the supply transformer the unbalanced currents as and when they occur.

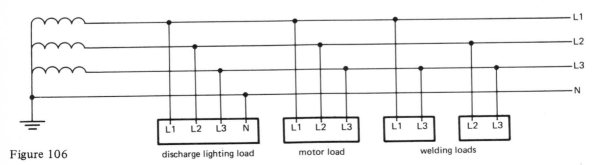

Figure 106   discharge lighting load   motor load   welding loads

197 (a) Explain briefly why temporary electrical installations on building sites should be designed to at least the same standard as permanent installations.

(b) For a temporary installation on a building site state the main requirements of the various regulations with regard to:

    (i)   type of switches to be used

    (ii) type of plugs and sockets

    (iii) use of overhead cables

    (iv) frequency of testing

(c) State *one* example in *each* case of plant or equipment connected to the following supply voltages:

    (i)   25 V single phase

    (ii)   110 V single phase

    (iii) 240 V single phase

    (iv) 415 V three phase   CGLI/II/83

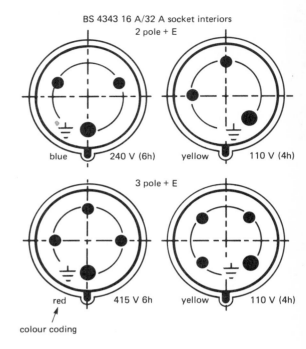

Figure 107

Solution

(a) In view of the nature of work and hazardous conditions on a building site, a temporary installation is much more vulnerable to misuse than a permanently connected installation. The system may be frequently changed and modified as work progresses and it is important to have a competent person in charge of it. The equipment and wiring systems used should therefore be inspected and tested periodically.

(b) (i) It is recommended that switches controlling single-phase supplies operating up to and including 110 V should be of the double-pole type with circuit protection provided in each live conductor. See BS CP 1017: 1969.

    (ii) Socket outlet and plugs should be designed to the standards of BS 4343 and should be either mechanically or electrically interlocked to ensure that the supply to the contact tubes of the accessory is isolated when the plug is withdrawn. Accessories are available for single and three-phase supplies with discrimination between different voltages by colour coding and the positioning of the earth contact in relation to a keyway (see examples in Figure 107).

    (iii) The use of overhead cables on a building site is not recommended but where it is unavoidable the minimum height of span above ground at road crossings is 5.8 m. In areas where mobile plant is prohibited, cables may be fixed at any height above 5.2 m. Such cables should be bound with tapes, yellow and black in accordance with BS 2929. See BS CP 1017: 1969.

    (iv) Temporary installations should be inspected and tested at regular three-month intervals. It is important for checks to be carried out on cable leads and portable tools and proper records kept of all site wiring and equipment.

(c) (i) Use of 25 V supply is suitable for damp and wet areas.

(ii) Use of 110 V supply is suitable for portable tools.

(iii) Use of 240 V supply is suitable for floodlighting.

(iv) Use of 415 V supply is suitable for large equipment, e.g. crane.

198 Show by means of a diagram the layout of a single-phase distribution system supplying outlet units for use on a construction site.

Solution

See Figure 109.

199 Show by means of a diagram a monitored earth protection system suitable for mobile plant on a construction site requiring a three-phase, 415 V supply.

Solution

See Figure 108. *Note* Students at Part II level are not required to draw this diagram.

200 (a) What are the requirements of the IEE Wiring Regulations regarding BS 1363 socket outlets on a ring final circuit?

(b) Draw a circuit diagram of a permanently connected appliance fed from a fused spur taken from a ring circuit.

Solution

(a) There are a number of requirements in the IEE Regulations – see Appendix 5.

(i) In domestic premises the floor area served must not exceed 100 m².

(ii) Consideration must be given to the loading of the circuit, particularly the loading in kitchens which may require a separate circuit.

(iii) An unlimited number of socket outlets may be provided. A twin or multiple socket outlet is regarded as one socket outlet.

(iv) The protective device at the origin of the circuit must be rated at 30–32 A and size of PVC insulated copper cables is 2.5 mm², PVC insulated copperclad aluminium is 4 mm² and MIMS copper cables is 1.5 mm².

(v) Immersion heaters and the like, in excess of 15 litres capacity should be supplied from their own circuits.

(vi) The number of non-fused spurs must not exceed the number of socket outlets and stationary equipment connected to the ring.

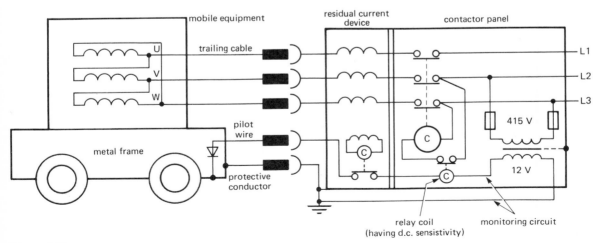

Figure 108

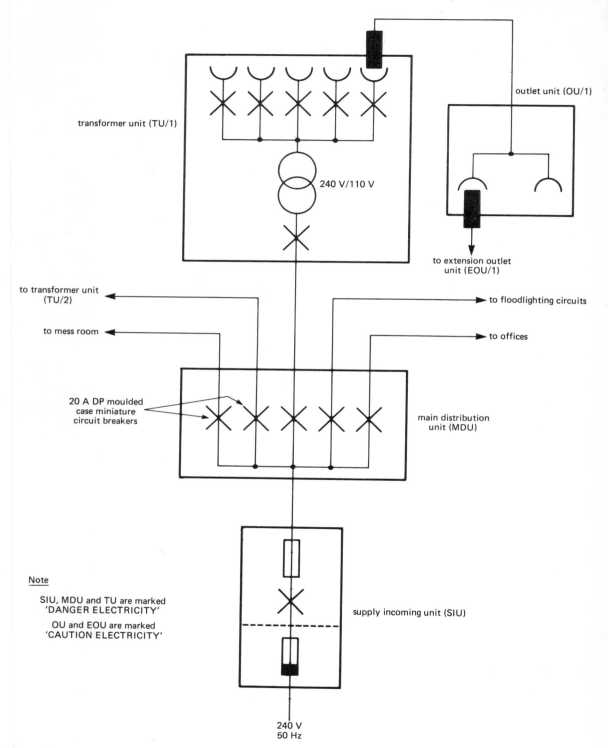

Figure 109

(vii) A non-fused spur must not feed more than one single or twin socket outlet, or more than one fixed appliance.

(viii) Permanently connected equipment must be fed from a fused spur rated at not more than 13 A and controlled by a switch or circuit breaker of rating not exceeding 16 A.

(b) See Figure 110.

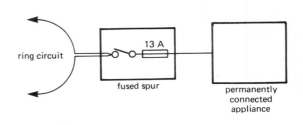